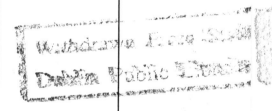

LAURENCE KING

Published in 2018 by
Laurence King Publishing
361–373 City Road
London EC1V 1LR
United Kingdom
T +44 20 7841 6900
F +44 20 7841 6910
enquiries@laurenceking.com
www.laurenceking.com

A catalogue record for this book is
available from the British Library.

*Read This if You Want to Be a Great
Writer* is based on an original concept
by Henry Carroll.

ISBN: 978 1 78627 197 6

Design: Rosa Nussbaum
Text research: Rachel Thorne
Photography: Ida Riveros

Printed in China

Contents

'Every story is — at the beginning — the same opening of a door onto a completely unknown space.'
—Margaret Atwood

The Seed

Every work of fiction grows from something. A thought. An image. A conversation in the supermarket. A fact. Sometimes, simply, the indefinable yearning to write something, even if you have no grasp of what it might be, or where that yearning is coming from.

From this seed, anything might grow – the realization of which can be daunting, and feel contrary to the way in which you perhaps plan and control your work, your life. But if you open yourself up to the unpredictability of what you might create, then it can also be liberating – and one of the most important skills that a writer learns is to embrace and use the potential of the unknown. You would be unlikely to start reading a book if you already knew every little thing about it, and the experiences of reading and writing are not so very far apart. They are entwined, in fact. It is important to remember that.

There are no rules. It is important to remember that, too. Every narrative is as individual as the person writing it. One of the quiet pleasures of writing fiction is that each project spawns its own storytelling rulebook – of language and style, of point of view, of character – which nobody but the author can impose.

There are, nonetheless, certain elements of craft to discover and to practise – to reject, sometimes – but, firstly, to understand.

'Prose is architecture,
not interior decoration.'
—Ernest Hemingway

First steps

Exploration
Planning
Research
Method
Form

Extracts of great writing

Lydia Davis: 'Swimming in Egypt'
Italo Calvino: *If on a Winter's Night a Traveler*

Exploration

You do not have to comprehend, at the outset, exactly what the thing you are going to write will turn into. So resist the temptation to fit your idea into a specific shape. The impulse to give order to your thoughts, your time, will become important at a later stage, but not yet. Now is the moment to experiment. To play.

It is common for beginning writers to approach a writing project in the same way that they are used to approaching a work or school project, striving for efficiency. Meticulous strategizing makes it feel more manageable: it makes it *look* more under control; it makes you think that you can forecast how long the project will take you. It can also make the whole business seem less indulgent. When your work colleagues, intrigued at your shift to part-time in order to write more, ask you what you did yesterday, it might feel easier to tell them, 'I drew up a chapter-by-chapter breakdown for a novel' than to say, 'I sat thinking for a couple of hours and ended up writing sort of a poem'.

Building up material is what, in turn, lets you build a plan.

Even though it may feel natural to devise an extensive plan first, which will then initiate the story, fiction writing, for most writers, works the other way round.

So, first of all, play around with the idea.

Keep a notebook, or use your phone to get down any thoughts that come to you when you are not at your desk striving to have thoughts. And make a note of anything — ideas, observations, images, conversations — even if they don't seem at the time to have much to do with the thing you are writing. They might well have something to do with the thing that you *end up* writing — or with something else that you write in the future.

Write random lines, passages, fragments, disconnected from any specific place in the text, immediately as they occur to you. (And note that it is once you free yourself from the burden of working to a fixed design that these things are more likely to occur to you.)

Use Post-it notes, a board, the floor ... anything that enables you to move things about and grow ideas in clusters. The eventual product will be linear in the sense that it will be one page followed by another, but your exploration of the idea does not have to be linear, and this method will help you to see associations forming, like a TV crime-evidence wall.

Play with form. Write a poem, draw a picture... Even if you are fairly sure that you are writing a novel, you will make important creative discoveries by crossing the borders between different means of expression.

Do some creative research. The most immobilizing thing you can do is to try and be in control, all the time, of the whole. If writer's block means anything, it means that. The time to be in control of the whole is at the end of the process, not at the beginning.

Planning

A plan, however, will be of use before you begin your first draft. For reassurance, if nothing else. The key is not to be beholden to it. Make multiple plans as you go along, and keep reinventing them throughout the project – they will gain traction as your word count increases.

The plan you draw up at the end of your first draft will have more value than any plan you make before the first draft.

Nevertheless, once you have amassed a horde of material, you may well be able to imagine some kind of vague plot shape, the sketching down of which could take any form you like.

A storyboard, for example, might look like the grid opposite. Or you could go for something looser, more hovering, like a spider diagram or a formative narrative map, such as the one on the following pages. The final two boxes of the storyboard, you will notice, have been left empty, as has the last part of the narrative map. You do not need to know how it ends yet (a line that I'm going to repeat throughout this book). Once you have a number of passages gathered together, and some narrative momentum going, you might *then* want to have a go at imagining a potential ending.

The rougher it is, the less you will feel obligated to fulfil it. Think of it as a prompt more than as an architectural blueprint. It could be that in sketching out a storyboard for what you had pictured as a novel, you realize that in fact you are more interested in writing a short story that is perfectly contained inside one of the boxes.

The narrative idea in the two sketches that follow is a simple one; a more abstract concept may call for a more abstract plan. Be creative. Allow for the possibility of new thoughts about the fiction even as you are laying down a plan.

1. An academically gifted teenager finishes her schooldays with a university place on offer and a bright future predicted for her by everyone.	2. An incidental visit to the doctor reveals that she has an illness, a debilitating one that before long may put her life in danger.
3. Not wanting to accept the truth of her situation, and fearful of letting everybody down, she makes the decision not to tell anybody about it.	4. Her condition worsens. She goes to great lengths to hide it from all around her.
5. She begins university. Another student takes a keen, increasingly menacing, interest in her. An uneasy relationship starts to form between the two.	6. A confrontation between them is followed, a few days later, by a malicious act secretively carried out against the main character.
7. to be continued....	8.

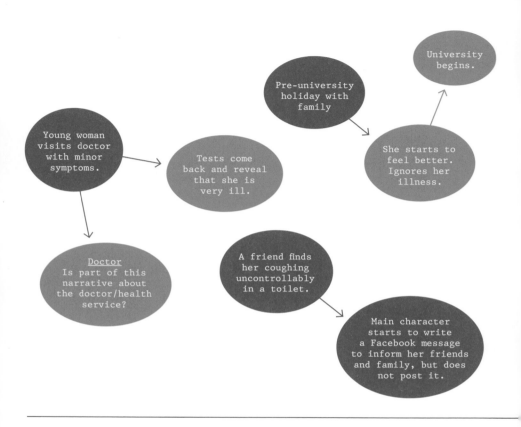

These are early-days sketches, yet they could start to give you the confidence that there might be a loose structure to work with. The fact that it is all contained on a sheet of paper is useful, as it precludes any inclination to use the plan as a reference bible. You can put it up on a wall, to glance at, rather than pore over in search of guidance. Furthermore, each of these plot ideas can act as a magnet for some of those loose fragments to pull towards. From here, you might be able to draft a scene or two, connected to any of these plot ideas...

Momentum is the crucial thing. A storyboard, a diagram, a napkin sketch, can help to generate that – even if, years later, you find it in a drawer and are amazed that this, once, had been your idea.

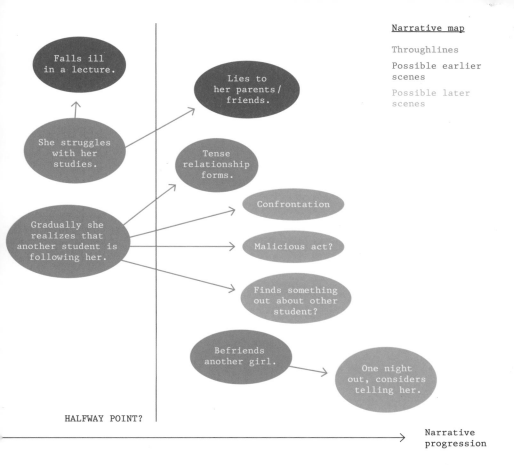

Narrative map

Throughlines

Possible earlier
scenes

Possible later
scenes

Falls ill
in a lecture.

Lies to
her parents/
friends.

She struggles
with her
studies.

Tense
relationship
forms.

Confrontation

Gradually she
realizes that
another student is
following her.

Malicious act?

Finds something
out about other
student?

Befriends
another girl.

One night
out, considers
telling her.

HALFWAY POINT?

Narrative
progression

The more material you build up, the more you will see the trace lines between things; the more your crime-wall shuffle will start to resemble a story – and the bigger your heap of paper will become, so now is a good time to organize that heap, into folders, binders, shoeboxes. This kind of thought ordering *is* beneficial, because it gives clarity to what has already started to form in your subconscious. And it brings new things to light. Even how you subdivide your heap of creative material can help give rise to new ideas. Especially if you are doing it with an eye on another heap of material that you have been building: research.

13

Research

It is tempting to think, 'Right, I am writing a short story about a trampoline artist, so what I'm going to do first is sit in front of my computer and Google the hell out of trampoline artists.'

However, you need to avoid thinking of factual research as a separate block of work from writing. The exploration of plot, character and language is more creatively engaged when it is *stimulated* by research, rather than built upon a foundation of research. The instinct to accumulate a knowledge base first, before being inventive, is another symptom of wanting to contain the beast. The more I know, the thought goes, the better I will be able to write about it, because I will have a wealth of accurate detail to call upon – and this is, to an extent, true – but ask yourself this question: What *is* research?

Think of research as a motor for your imagination. Fact-finding can certainly feed your imagination – as can a number of other actions. But research, viewed more broadly than just knowledge build-up, can take myriad forms, which, crucially, should be done at different times.

Research is a creative venture, too.

The technique of 'spaced learning', whereby intense study bursts are punctuated by short intervals of a contrasting activity, has been found to greatly improve students' ability to absorb information, and you can use a similar mental process as you garner details and background knowledge for the world of your fiction. Be fluid in your research process: rather than burying your head in a book for an afternoon, swap frequently between the different research angles outlined over the next few pages to allow space for new inspiration to embed itself. And make writing part of your spacing activity, too. Move repeatedly between reading and listening and looking and writing. Get all the cogs turning at the same time.

Avoid aimless surfing	Trawling the internet may motivate you for a while, but soon enough you will get lost, and drift further and further from whatever it was that first excited you and prompted you to write. So use the internet sparingly for now (it will become very important at other stages) and try to look at your subject from as many other angles as possible.
Broaden your search	Don't just look at text. To rely solely upon the written word as a source of material is limiting, because you are in the imaginative slipstream of somebody else's use of language. So consider other artistic treatments of the subject, too: photography, film, visual and conceptual art, theatre, television, music, dance, graphic novels, architecture... The benefit is that the edges of the subject you think you are researching become blurred, which allows you to learn more and, even more importantly, imagine more.
Don't ring-fence your idea	Begin by researching one area of study, but allow yourself to deviate. This is the same principle as discussed under Exploration on page 8 – not boxing off your idea before it has had the chance to grow into something. If, while researching, you happen to discover a subject that animates you, the likelihood is that it could animate your writing, so don't avoid it simply because you've already decided that you know what you are writing about. If a conversation with a woman about forcing rhubarb ends up not going in your trampoline artist story, so what? You don't need to know all the answers until you've finished, remember. The best creative ideas are often the ones you are not looking for.

And if the newly discovered subject has sprung from studying the original subject, it's probably not going to be too far off the mark anyway. Maybe the trampoline artist likes forcing rhubarb too.

There is a caveat here, of course: to allow yourself this deviating impulse away from the internet. Which brings us to arguably the most valuable kind of research.

People

Speak to as many real human beings as you can about your subject. Ask them questions and let them talk... You will find out things that you did not expect to find out, and as for most writers (at least those who have an interest in characters), real-life people are more likely to inspire you than the internet.

Different types of fiction writing require different types, and amounts, of conversation. So think about what conversations might help your own project. If you are writing about a fishing community in Grimsby in the 1970s, go to Grimsby and speak to people there. Record these conversations, if the interviewee is comfortable with you doing so. When you play back your recording, study the voices – the words, the cadence, the humour – transcribe them, experiment with the words on a page.

Invention

Not all research is based on the real. The fabric of a fictional narrative weaves material that has come from the real world with material that has come from the writer. Let yourself be creative from the get-go. Your fiction will be richer if you create your invented histories, plot lines and character stories while you are still thinking about the factual research you did the day before – and vice versa.

Furthermore, try other art forms. Looking at a book of photographs of 1970s Grimsby is going to be useful for that fishing community novel; so is taking your own photographs, surrounding your workspace with them to glance at while you are writing, triggering the sensory memory of the moment when you took the shot: the smell of fish in tubs, the texture of a hull...

Getting it right

There is a time for meticulously researching what all the different parts of a fishing vessel are called, or the most popular dog names in Australia at the turn of the century, but that time is very rarely during, or before, the first draft. The above types of research can be done in and around your exploration of the fiction idea, but don't get hung up on exacting detail at the outset because it will impede your creative momentum, and will probably be symptomatic of you shying away from getting on with writing. The time for filler detail is during a later draft, or an edit (see the chapters on Method and Editing). Which is when, finally, the internet really is your friend.

It is worth pointing out that all of the above (and everything in this book so far) applies, in my eyes, to both novel and short-story writing. Naturally enough, a short story will usually involve less research than a novel – but there may be exceptions. It will always depend on the individual project. A particular kind of abstract, placeless novel, for example, might require less factual research than a short story about a trampoline artist. It may well, however, warrant a greater amount of invention and appetite-whetting research.

> Start writing before you think you know everything.

The other advantage of not doing all your research as one block at the beginning is that you are more likely to actually begin writing. Don't wait for the assurance that you are really absolutely profoundly ready to begin the writing bit. Just get writing.

Method

As much as we might enjoy hearing apocryphal stories of famous authors' quirks – that Joyce wrote in bed in a white coat; that Joan Didion sleeps beside her manuscript so that it doesn't leave her; that Dan Brown hangs upside down in anti-gravity boots – they make no difference to the reader's enjoyment of that author's book. The important thing, as an author, is to know what ritual, eccentric or not, works for you.

If this means that you do your best writing when you are naked in the bathtub is for you to discover. As is, crucially, the method by which you develop an idea into a finished piece of writing. Every writer has their own process. I have put down in this chapter some of the main ways in which writers go about creating a piece of fiction. You will notice, however diverse they may at first appear, that there is a lot of crossover, and that most of them involve some kind of milling process.

> **Nothing comes out perfectly first time.**

The relative weight I have given to the first method is because it contains many of the basic principles, and, possibly, because it is the way in which I work myself. I should add that I work in the same way for both novels and short stories. But it is not for me to prescribe the most effective process, and you will inevitably consider some of these methods barmy; others may strike a chord, or you might take titbits from all of them. The only way for you to discover your own method is to experiment, and to write – and complete – as much as you can. And to remember, always, that there is no *correct* way to write but your own.

The refinery method

With a formative idea and a loose plan, embark on a linear first draft. Work from some semblance of a beginning – without stopping to doubt yourself, make improvements, or judge the writing – to an end. The only judgements you should make are instinctive creative ones: Is this character starting to feel more significant than I had envisaged? The storyline seems to have deviated from my plan ... but what might happen if I go down this new path? Is the point of view serving the story I want to tell? How does it feel if I change it for a chapter or two?

> The point of this rough drafting is to remove the pressure of a polished product.

Rough exploratory drafting is an antidote to the anxiety of the blank page. You are generating momentum, a rhythm to your thoughts and your accumulating scenes, even if the actual text you are producing is – or would be if this was going to be the finished manuscript – a hilarious piece of crap. Overwritten in most places, underwritten in others; a tense change halfway through; plot lines and characters abandoned, or appearing from nowhere. But, by the end of it (which will probably not be the right ending), you will have a very good idea of what works and what doesn't, because you have learned these things through experimentation.

And this is the point at which to write it again.

The second draft begins on a clean page. Very possibly in a different place to where the first draft began, because it is quite likely that you wrote a scene partway through the first draft that suggested itself to you later as an appropriate opening. The process of redrafting is not one of simply copying out the best bits from the first-draft material (although it will sometimes involve doing that). It is a *new* piece of writing; one that you are commencing with a deep understanding, now, of your idea, style, characters, plot, and with at least some decent lines and scenes in the bank.

How you make use of the first-draft material is for you to decide: whether you have written a mess of longhand that you now take a highlighter or a number of coloured pens to; whether you refer to it closely, chapter by chapter, or barely refer to it at all; whether you complete two full drafts, or more, or redraft certain areas of it more than others.

Whatever way you go about it, the process does not end here. The redraft does not produce the finished piece of writing, so, still, you should not feel the pressure of it being a finished piece of writing. The final part of this method is the edit (which we will come to on page 124).

If you have not yet thoroughly worked out your method, then this may all feel rather painstaking to you, but it is a question of care. Ask yourself: 'How much do I care about my writing?' And consider too, that the more defined your method, the more defined the final product is likely to be.

The jigsaw method	If you are stumped for the point at which to enter the narrative it may be helpful to forego, for now, an adherence to writing it in a linear way, from beginning to end. Instead, if you do have an idea for one or two scenes that feel pertinent, even though you don't know where exactly they fit, then start with those. The more you write, the better you will understand the project at large. And you may, eventually, understand that the finished narrative will not be linear. It might, for example, be episodic.

So, by writing a big scene that eventually ends up at the core of the narrative, you will be growing your understanding of the fictional world and the characters who inhabit it – and this, in turn, is likely to spawn other ideas, other scenes, character through-lines, plot events. Once you free yourself from the constraint of putting it down in the right order, you may well find that before very long you have gathered enough fragments that you are beginning to get a perception of the whole.

The nugget in the dump method	This is another variation on the first, and a further relinquishing of control. You cannot know for sure, before you have amassed any words, whether this thing you are writing is worthwhile. Which is why it is so tempting to plan it into an impressive shape, to convince yourself that it is. Your first draft is an exploration. During that exploration you might unearth a completely unexpected idea, character, sentence that causes you to think: actually, *this* is the thing that has legs.

So the first draft of one book might be what instigates the first draft of a different book.

Maybe the idea of discarding a whole draft sounds demoralizing – and so it might be, for a while – but is it as demoralizing as knowing that you have spent years writing something that is not as good, as impassioned, as the idea that you left behind?

The spurt method

Some writers sit at a desk for hours and work without pause until their designated time to punch the clock. I am one of these. Others, like Nick Hornby, write in spurts. A few sentences at a time, then a short break to get up and stretch their limbs before returning to it, refreshed. If you feel that you work best by keeping office hours, keep office hours, but don't do so just to make your writing feel more legitimate.

Plenty of writers set themselves word targets, and you might find it helpful to have a number to aim for each day. However, don't let yourself be crippled by it – either your own target, or another writer's. Anthony Trollope made himself write 250 words every fifteen minutes, timing himself with a stopwatch. Fair enough. You don't have to. The reader is not bothered about how long it took you.

The sessional method

In order to create momentum, you might find it helpful to vary what you do, session by session. So, you might spend one session drafting a scene, and the next session rewriting that scene. Furthermore – and this is a useful thing to bear in mind, whatever your method – you might grease the wheels of your stopping-and-starting routine by drawing a close to your writing session at a point where you know what is going to come next on the page. As Hemingway put it: 'As long as you can start, you are alright. The juice will come.'

You might, furthermore, heed Hemingway's advice on rereading what you have done so far, to get into the flow of the material. There are, believe it or not, plenty of writers who will reread the whole draft up to the point they've got to, each time they sit down to write. Or, if you are Hemingway, stand.

The perfectionist method

At the opposite end of the spectrum from the process of generating momentum through drafting is the process of refining each individual page, over and over, before you move on to the next page. In this way, every existing page is in its final state as the narrative continues, and the end of the work really does mean the end of the work. It is a practice of constant revision, rather than redrafting. Anthony Burgess worked in this way, in part because he believed that over time the intention and technique of a writer is liable to change, with the result that the unity of the work will be affected.

The incubation method

Although I have been advocating getting pen to paper as early as possible, there are writers who let an idea remain in their heads for a long time. They will ruminate at length, letting the subconscious stay constantly engaged with the subject so that characters, plot and atmosphere form without any forced deliberation. In this way, seemingly incongruent observations and encounters from the author's day-to-day life feed into the thought process.

All the while, it will be important to keep a notebook, to write down any scraps that occur to you – until, eventually, you have what is in effect a first draft in the imagination. It will be amorphous, but the putting together of all your notes (maybe even writing them down on record cards that you can then lay out on a table) will create a vague shape for you to use when you do sit down to write.

It has a resemblance, this method, to the act of reading: you immerse yourself inside a dreamed world, in which you are capable of imagining characters doing more than simply what is written down. The trick, I suppose, is knowing when to stop dreaming and get down to it.

Form

'I am going to write a novel', you might have told yourself.
The certainty of this is reassuring. You know what a novel
looks like. As a physical object, you can picture it. But what if
your idea, you begin to wonder, would better suit a short story?
Or a novella? What, actually, even *is* a novella?

It will be realism, though, you are sure about that. Although,
in truth, many of the early fragments you have written don't
feel very realistic at all, except for the bits that draw so heavily
from your own experience that you think they might in fact be
memoir. Maybe, then, you could call what you are doing
autofiction, because everybody seems to be going nuts for
that these days. So you Google Knausgaard, and realize that you
still don't really understand what autofiction means.

Many of the labels that are used to categorize different kinds
of fiction – flash fiction, novella, science fiction, speculative
fiction, literary fiction, YA, thriller, etc. – are just that: labels.

Often, they will have been applied to the work after its
completion, by somebody other than the author. It is not unusual
for an author never to have considered that their narrative
was of a particular type while they were writing it. It's not
unusual, either, for an author to disagree with the commercial
classification that their work has been shelved under. They
were just writing the thing that they wanted to write. And that,
fundamentally, is a pretty decent way of going about it.

The more words you write, the more material you draft, the clearer it will become what shape the thing might eventually take.

If, before you have even put pen to paper, you have already convinced yourself that this will be a novel, or this will be realism, or this will be a comic social-protest short story, you are at once placing a burden of expectation, and commitment, upon yourself that may well make it difficult to start. If instead you tell yourself, 'this *might* be a novel, but let's see where the idea leads me', you will probably find it much easier to get going. Commitment is vital for any writer – but commitment to the idea, to your craft, not to some idealized instruction that you have foisted upon yourself.

An idea does not necessarily slot into only one box, either. The idea that you have for a short story might well also work for a novel, and vice versa. The treatment and focus of that idea would clearly take different paths, and at some point you would obviously need to make a decision about which way you were going to go. Making those choices, those discoveries, is part of the enjoyment of writing fiction. Give yourself the freedom for an idea to morph into something you didn't expect it to; the freedom, too, to let yourself turn away from any preconceptions you may have. There is no value in slogging away at a novel that you know, but dare not admit, would have been more interesting if you'd let it become a short story.

> Let the *writing* inform any choices of form and genre that need to be made.

For some contemporary authors, autobiography is the direction in which art has been and should be heading. Autofiction – the blending together of fiction and autobiography – is not a new concept. The term has been in use since the 1970s, when the French writer Serge Doubrovsky came up with it when describing his own novel, *Fils*, but writers such as Karl Ove Knausgaard, Rachel Cusk and Édouard Louis have in recent years brought the form to a new attention.

Autofiction is a purposeful pushing down on one side of the scales (autobiography) in rejection of the other (artificially constructed fiction, namely realism). It stems from the belief that fabricated characters and plot are excruciatingly fake: why falsely contrive made-up characters into scenes to then act out the author's point, when you could just have the character – who might be the author, or somebody the author has met – make the point directly?

Autofiction has its limitations, as any form does: the range of possibilities of structure, tone and point of view are consciously narrow; it has the potential to hurt or anger real people who can identify themselves in the narrative; and if the writing is not extremely good, it can give the feeling of somebody incessantly talking about him- or herself.

Probing, questioning, form is part of the writer's job.

What the form does do, however, is challenge preconceived notions of what fiction is supposed to look like.

When form is bent into something new, your previously programmed way of reading a text can be, too.

If you are specifically targeting the work at a market, make sure that you properly understand your motivation for doing so. Do you think that your book is YA simply because it is about a group of teenagers? Wouldn't Old Adults also enjoy reading a book about young people? Is it 'women's fiction' because there are women in it, or because you are a woman? Can any book, for that matter, reasonably be categorized as women's fiction if there is not also a shelf of books called 'men's fiction'?

Always question the labels. Understand them, challenge and have fun with them. Developing your knowledge of a particular genre – its conventions of structure, theme, character – so that you know the specific effects that can be achieved within it, is a much better way of serving your idea than incuriously sticking to a template. That way you are more likely to make use of what the genre can do well, or ride against the conventions to create something new. And creating something new should always be your intention. Even if the work turns into a prime example of a particular type of writing, it nonetheless should be adding to what already exists. Something about it – the story, or the way in which the story is told – should be original. Fiction is a place that people go to have new thoughts. There are lots of other places for the regurgitation of old ones.

Some works of fiction that play with preconceived notions of what fiction is supposed to look like can be so compelling that they create their own market. When form is bent into something new, your previously programmed way of reading a text can be, too.

> There are enough mechanisms to simplify and stereotype books and readers out there already without you needing to add to them.

**What is a
short story?**

There has been much ballyhoo over the categorization of Lydia Davis's short fiction. Much of it, like this piece, takes the form of a single paragraph, less than a page in length – sometimes only a few lines. 'Flash fiction', some say. Meditations. Prose poems. This compulsion to explain them away is, I think, partly a reaction to the discomfiting experience of reading them. Without the recognizable structures of a known form, the stories throb with a vague, vulnerable intensity. In the same way that a dream does. (It is not a coincidence that many of the stories are tagged as having originated from a dream.)

In 'Swimming in Egypt', we follow the narrative voice through the water and the tunnel – and at the sudden drop into the open sea we too feel the exposure, the fragility, of being. The piece is a tiny pearl of existential awe; the tension between liberated freedom and the restraint of being careful to 'find our way back to the mouth of the tunnel'.

You could write a longer short story with that thematic idea. Or a novel. Those longer forms, though, would find it difficult to sustain the floating ambiguous mood that is brought about by the use of the first-person plural, while not explaining who 'we' are, or providing any contextual grip whatsoever.

And so, perhaps, stories like this one, stripped of a conventional sequence of events, of characters with motivations and backstories, are closer to what life is actually like for most of us a lot of the time: unexpected, oblique, banal, hard to explain.

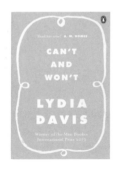

'Swimming in
Egypt' from
Can't and Won't
Lydia Davis
2014

Swimming in Egypt

We are in Egypt. We are about to go deep-sea diving. They have erected a vast tank of water on land next to the Mediterranean Sea. We strap oxygen to our backs and descend into this tank. We go all the way to the bottom. Here, there is a cluster of blue lights shining on the entrance to a tunnel. We enter the tunnel. The tunnel will lead into the Mediterranean. We swim and swim. At the far end of the tunnel, we see more lights, white ones. When we have passed through the lights, we come out of the tunnel, suddenly, into the open sea, which drops away beneath us a full kilometer or more. There are fish all around and above us, and reefs on all sides. We think we are flying, over the deep. We forget, for now, that we must be careful not to get lost, but must find our way back to the mouth of the tunnel.

dream

What is a novel?

There is a frisky charge of humour that comes from stepping off the tracks – while still conscious of where the tracks are supposed to be. *If on a Winter's Night a Traveler* begins by immediately blurring the familiar demarcations of author, narrator and reader, turning 'you' into a slippery amalgamation of all three. In so doing, the question of 'What is fiction?' is straightaway brought into the open.

The novel is made up of multiple layers: of author identity and reader identity, of metafiction (fiction about fiction), and of a series of interlocked narratives. The book is a Russian doll of narratives, in fact: there are a dozen different openings to novels in it, each written in a different style. So, we begin a detective novel, a romance, a satire, an erotic adventure … each one broken off just as it is getting going. And at the hub of them all is that second-person 'you', the author/reader hybrid, desperately chasing the ever-escaping story. But will you ever be able to catch up with it, look it in the eye and say 'Aha! Now I have you'? Or will you forever find yourself shedding skins, searching and searching? Perhaps the only thing that is certain is that it is very difficult to write about *If on a Winter's Night a Traveler* without slipping into the style of it.

The shape-shifting form of this novel makes us think about the act of reading: both the physical act of it and also the mental bargain that we are customarily expected to make when we pick up a work of fiction. We *know* that what is being described is not real, but at the same time we are prepared to suspend our disbelief to behave as if it were:

> 'Of course, the ideal position for reading is something you can never find.'

If on a Winter's Night a Traveler
Italo Calvino
1980

Chapter One

You are about to begin reading Italo Calvino's new novel, *If on a winter's night a traveler*. Relax. Concentrate. Dispel every other thought. Let the world around you fade. Best to close the door; the TV is always on in the next room. Tell the others right away, "No, I don't want to watch TV!" Raise your voice — they won't hear you otherwise — "I'm reading! I don't want to be disturbed!" Maybe they haven't heard you, with all that racket; speak louder, yell: "I'm beginning to read Italo Calvino's new novel!" Or if you prefer, don't say anything; just hope they'll leave you alone.

Find the most comfortable position: seated, stretched out, curled up, or lying flat. Flat on your back, on your side, on your stomach. In an easy chair, on the sofa, in the rocker, the deck chair, on the hassock. In the hammock, if you have a hammock. On top of your bed, of course, or in the bed. You can even stand on your hands, head down, in the yoga position. With the book upside down, naturally.

Of course, the ideal position for reading is something you can never find. In the old days they used to read standing up, at a lectern. People were accustomed to standing on their feet, without moving. They rested like that when they were tired of horseback riding. Nobody ever thought of reading on horseback; and yet now, the idea of sitting in the saddle, the book propped against the horse's mane, or maybe tied to the horse's ear with a special harness, seems attractive to you. With your feet in the stirrups, you should feel quite comfortable for reading; having your feet up is the first condition for enjoying a read.

'Fiction tells you,
by making up of truth,
what really is true.'
—Ali Smith

Chapter Two

Technique

The opening
Characters
Place
Point of view
Language
Plot
Dialogue
Sex
Originality

Extracts of great writing

Carson McCullers: *The Heart is a Lonely Hunter*
Antonio Tabucchi: *Pereira Maintains*
Alice Munro: 'The Beggar Maid'
James Joyce: 'A Mother'
Claire Keegan: *Walk the Blue Fields*
Raymond Carver: 'Where I'm Calling From'
Thomas Hardy: *The Return of the Native*
Sarah Hall: *The Carhullan Army*
A. M. Homes: *May We Be Forgiven*
Charles Dickens: *Bleak House*
James Kelman: *Dirt Road*
Saul Bellow: *Herzog*
Peter Carey: *True History of the Kelly Gang*
Jhumpa Lahiri: 'Interpreter of Maladies'
Doris Lessing: *The Grass is Singing*
Evan S. Connell: *Mrs Bridge*
Zadie Smith: *On Beauty*
Patrick McCabe: *The Butcher Boy*
Nell Zink: *The Wallcreeper*
Eimear McBride: *A Girl is a Half-Formed Thing*
Muriel Spark: *The Driver's Seat*
Javier Marías: *A Heart So White*

The opening

Why include a chapter on the opening? Is there a unique importance to the first sentence, the first paragraph, the first page, that is deserving of special attention? In short: no, there is not.

The reason, in fact, for including a chapter on openings is primarily to argue the point that there is no need for a chapter on openings.

There is a popular presumption that the first page of a work of fiction must 'grab the reader's attention'. Which is, in essence, true. However, the idea that it should do so by being loaded with superficial appeal is misleading. You might hear some publishers and agents advocate making sure that your opening stands out. Even authors sometimes say this. A novelist gave a talk to a group of my students recently and recommended that they put their most impressive sentences on the first page. I would say to you, as I said to my students, that this advice is best ignored. It patronizes readers to presume that they are so easily bored, that the internet has contracted our attention spans to the extent that making a decision about whether or not to read more than a page of a book is akin to thumbing through Tinder. The effect of giving a special status to the opening is twofold:

Disjointedness occurs, because of a stylistic, or dramatic, separation from the rest of the narrative.

The author becomes visible.

What makes for a 'good' opening is not its clever distinction from the rest of the text; it is the ease with which we are pulled inside the invented world – what John Gardner termed 'the fictional dream'. I do not read in order to imagine the writer at a desk, pen in hand, mid-century Danish chaise longue in the corner, crafting the perfect metaphor.

Not that there is anything wrong with a finely tuned metaphor, but every sentence on that first page should be there because it belongs to the whole, not because of a fear that without the inducement of shiny baubles the reader will put the book down and walk away. It is the promise of the whole, the enticing mystery of it, that makes us stay – so at the root of any reader's compulsion to read beyond the first page is, naturally, intrigue.

> I read in order to be transported, to disappear. The author's goal should be to do the same.

Whether we consider the opening to be the first sentence, the first page or the first chapter, it should be possible to distil from it a question, or multiple questions, which the reader hungers to answer. This might be as blunt as 'Who killed the postman?' Or it might, like the two examples we are about to see, come in diverse and subtle ways.

No nonsense

It is the simplicity of this opening that draws us in. No shiny baubles are on display here. The guiding steadiness of the narrative voice evokes a mood of oral storytelling: 'In the town there were two mutes', 'The two friends were very different', 'The one who… The other…', 'Then when they came to a certain fruit and candy store…'. There is a neat containment to the arrangement of sentences, which heightens the atmosphere of orderliness and stability. Notice, too, that the only sentence that does away with the syntactic exactitude of the main – 'In the summer he would come out wearing a yellow or green polo shirt stuffed sloppily into his trousers in front and hanging loose behind' – does so purposely, leaving out any commas to give the impression of the Greek's shabby clothing. Singer, by contrast, is dressed by the clipped plainness of description of his appearance: 'The other mute was tall. His eyes had a quick, intelligent expression. He was always immaculate and very soberly dressed.'

There is a lovely potency to the echoing use of 'always'. Especially, when describing Singer's placing a hand on his friend's arm, the one instance in which it is qualified by '*nearly always*'. Those two simple words manage effortlessly to capture how longstanding, how continuous, how – if this is the minute level at which some variation to the routine might show itself – unwavering this relationship is. Very subtly, a narrative tension is brought about as we realize (helped on by the past-tense storytelling, which gives the text the natural inflection of this time being over) that the constancy of this bond between the two men has the potential to be broken.

The Heart Is
a Lonely Hunter
Carson McCullers
1940

PART ONE

In the town there were two mutes, and they were always together. Early every morning they would come out from the house where they lived and walk arm in arm down the street to work. The two friends were very different. The one who always steered the way was an obese and dreamy Greek. In the summer he would come out wearing a yellow or green polo shirt stuffed sloppily into his trousers in front and hanging loose behind. When it was colder he wore over this a shapeless grey sweater. His face was round and oily, with half-closed eyelids and lips that curved in a gentle, stupid smile. The other mute was tall. His eyes had a quick, intelligent expression. He was always immaculate and very soberly dressed.

Every morning the two friends walked silently together until they reached the main street of the town. Then when they came to a certain fruit and candy store they paused for a moment on the sidewalk outside. The Greek, Spiros Antonapoulos, worked for his cousin, who owned this fruit store. His job was to make candies and sweets, uncrate the fruits, and to keep the place clean. The thin mute, John Singer, nearly always put his hand on his friend's arm and looked for a second into his face before leaving him. Then after this good-bye Singer crossed the street and walked on alone to the jewellery store where he worked as a silverware engraver.

In the late afternoon the friends would meet again. Singer came back to the fruit store and waited until Antonapoulos was ready to go home. The Greek would be lazily unpacking a case of peaches or melons, or perhaps looking at the funny paper in the kitchen behind the store where he cooked.

**The one-
word tease**

Ask yourself: 'At what point have I slipped inside the fictional
dream?'

I am there at once, transported directly into sunny Lisbon
by the limpid ease of that first line. The language is as crisp and
clear as the sky outside Pereira's window – yet what impels us
onwards is the choice of one word: 'maintains'. This single word
underpins the whole novel with intrigue and tension. To whom
does Pereira have to justify himself? To the mysterious presence
narrating his tale? To himself? To an authority? The word is
repeated, like an incantation, so often that it begins to structure
the narrative – and observe how the effect of reiteration in
general forms a backdrop to the text, lulling us inside it, like
the lapping of waves onto the shore:

> 'Pereira maintains he met him one summer's day. A fine
> fresh sunny summer's day'

> 'a city glittering, literally glittering'

A kind of rhetorical wooing is going on here, one that,
you might begin to sense, feels reminiscent of the courtroom.

There is the suggestion of surface – 'sparkling', 'glittering'
– underwritten by the natural counterweight of what might
lie beneath. This idea, too, has a parallel – in the relationship
between timeframes: the 'fresh sunny day' of the present; the
difficulties of Pereira's past (and notice how much natural
backstory is layered in, about his father, his wife's death, his
doctor's prognosis); and, most ominously, the even greater
implicit difficulties of the future.

There is nothing static about either this novel's opening or
that of *The Heart is a Lonely Hunter*. We are cast directly into
a moving story, in which the characters are already in action.
There is no explanatory release of how McCullers' two
friends' mutism developed, or why Pereira has to substantiate
his version of the truth. These things are left to the intrigue
of our imaginations.

Pereira Maintains
Antonio Tabucchi
2010

1

Pereira maintains he met him one summer's day. A fine fresh sunny summer's day and Lisbon was sparkling. It would seem that Pereira was in his office biting his pen, the editor-in-chief was away on holiday while he himself was saddled with getting together the culture page, because the *Lisboa* was now to have a culture page and he had been given the job. But he, Pereira, was meditating on death. On that beauteous summer day, with the sun beaming away and the sea-breeze off the Atlantic kissing the treetops, and a city glittering, literally glittering beneath his window, and a sky of such a blue as never was seen, Pereira maintains, and of a clarity almost painful to the eyes, he started to think about death. Why so? Pereira cannot presume to say. Maybe because when he was little his father owned an undertaker's establishment with the gloomy name of Pereira La Dolorosa, maybe because his wife had died of consumption some years before, maybe because he was fat and suffered from heart trouble and high blood pressure and the doctor had told him that if he went on like this he wouldn't last long. But the fact is that Pereira began dwelling on death, he maintains. And by chance, purely by chance, he started leafing through a magazine. It was a literary review, though with a section devoted to philosophy. Possibly an avant-garde review, Pereira is not definite on this point, but with a fair share of Catholic contributors. And Pereira was a Catholic, or at least at that moment he felt himself a Catholic, a good Roman Catholic, though there was one thing he could not bring himself to believe in, and that was the resurrection of the body.

However the intrigue is formed, it is usually related to the reader's innate tendency to want to understand the 5 Ws – a principle of puzzle-solving recognizable to police investigators, journalists, researchers, and to rhetoricians as far back as Cicero:

Who are these characters?
Just who are those two mutes? Who is Pereira maintaining his story to? And bear in mind that this intrigue refers not just to the characters on the page, but also potentially to characters off the page: Who is narrating the events of this story? To what implied audience, and why – what is their motivation for telling it?

What is going on?

Where is it taking place?

When? Is it now or in the past – or in the future? And is the telling of the story taking place at the same time as the story itself, or is there a separation between the two: is it told from a distance?

Why are the characters behaving as they are – and, crucially, what will be the consequences of this behaviour?

Once you appreciate that the opening to your piece of fiction has this web of potential intrigue already latent within it, you can release yourself from the pressure to make your first page cry 'Look at me!' Carefully mould the 5 Ws. Don't make them so immediately answerable that the reader's intrigue flatlines; equally, don't make it all so confusing that the reader cannot develop an interest. Give your reader something to get their chops around. Let them into the dream.

Characters

Characters are the lifeblood of fiction. They are primary to our understanding of and our emotional response to a narrative. We can all think of characters from our reading past that have stayed with us, moved us, altered our perception of the world – and we can probably also come up with reasons why those particular characters affect us so much. There is, however, no useful, honest, general guide to the creation of compelling characters, precisely because characters are themselves individuated. Which, in essence, is the most important characteristic of every character you will ever write.

Each character, much like the work of fiction he or she inhabits, is unique.

This is, I would argue, as true of a character who appears in only a single sentence as it is of a central protagonist who is present on every page of a 300,000-word novel. Even if we glimpse only a fragment of the life of a character, we should still be able to imaginatively grasp the whole of that life. I have never thought of bit-part characters as having a function, a one-note role to play – E. M. Forster's theory of 'flat' characters, easily recognizable types who carry the purpose of a joke or a plot point in their orbiting of 'round' characters, the major players. I believe that if you think of any character as a device, so will your reader. You cannot design a character, of any size, to fit the story. Writing good fiction is not as conveniently neat as that. Characters *are* the story. To calculate and project them onto a narrative before actually starting to write their stories is a bit like sellotaping swatch samples to an expanse of wall that you intend to paint. You never really know how it's all going to work out until you begin colouring it in.

Because capturing the full intensity of a life can seem like a pretty daunting task, it may well feel tempting to break down your approach to character creation into a set of considerations: this is the character's inner conflict; this is what the character looks like; this is the character's family, education, class, romantic background; this is what they might have in their pockets; and so on. The shortcoming to thinking about characterization as the management of constituent parts, though, is that they turn into different variations of the same building blocks, like Lego figures.

This is where drafting comes in. You may well write many pages of a first draft that are later discarded, but the writing of those pages will develop your knowledge of characters, so that even if some specific events and motivations and backstories do not find their way into the eventual text, the underlying energy of them will. Furthermore, developing characters on the page of a draft, rather than in a notebook, will engender greater complexity than a simple flat/round distinction. Characters who you might at first have imagined to be central, and given thousands of first-draft words to, might in the final reckoning appear only in passing – in a sentence that carries the import of all that imagining you have already done. Or, a character you once thought would be peripheral might grow into the lead.

> A fictional character only comes alive on the page.

It's all very well knowing what's in their pockets, but it is language that will animate them. So put the sketchbook down and get writing. Get the characters moving with *words*.

As a first example of characterization, let's assess the opening of 'The Beggar Maid', by Alice Munro.

**Flipping
the focus**

'The Beggar Maid' begins, tellingly, not with the main character,
Rose, but instead: 'Patrick Blatchford was in love with Rose.'
This simple flip of focus gives us, already, a sense of Rose's
character, her passivity. Look at the controlling force of those
three early sentences in a row that begin with 'He'. Rose lacks
agency because she is being directed, not only by other people,
but by the sentences themselves. It is noticeable, even in these
two pages, how few of the sentences concerning Rose's thoughts
and actions begin with 'Rose' or 'She' – in comparison to
Patrick, or even Dr Henshawe's, sentences.

There is comic effect drawn from this technique too,
in the characterization of Patrick: ('he ... spilled drinks and
bowls of peanuts, like a comedian. He was not a comedian...
He came from British Columbia.') These observations are
Rose's, tentatively offered, and when the real character of Rose
does start to emerge more clearly, it does so with parentheses,
mischievous asides, like an internal whispering:

'(Something did cancel them out, or at least diminish
them, for her; she had to keep reminding herself they
were there.)'

The early, striking, use of the word 'furious' to describe
Patrick's love serves to imbue the narrative with a combative
edge that belongs to him, not to Rose. Her own identity is
given little room, at this point in the story, the language of
which is possessed by both Patrick and also – as is a trait of
Alice Munro's stories – by a vernacular of place, of small-town
Canada. That word 'tarty', in reference to the silver sandals
Rose buys, encapsulates brilliantly the delicate balance of
Rose's life: between poverty and privilege, her past and her
present; between languages.

'The Beggar Maid'
from *The Beggar
Maid: Stories
of Flo and Rose*
Alice Munro
1996

THE BEGGAR MAID

Patrick Blatchford was in love with Rose. This had become a fixed, even furious, idea with him. For her, a continual surprise. He wanted to marry her. He waited for her after classes, moved in and walked beside her, so that anybody she was talking to would have to reckon with his presence. He would not talk, when these friends or classmates of hers were around, but he would try to catch her eye, so that he could indicate by a cold incredulous look what he thought of their conversation. Rose was flattered, but nervous. A girl named Nancy Falls, a friend of hers, mispronounced Metternich in front of him. He said to her later, "How can you be friends with people like that?"

Nancy and Rose had gone and sold their blood together, at Victoria Hospital. They each got fifteen dollars. They spent most of the money on evening shoes, tarty silver sandals. Then because they were sure the bloodletting had caused them to lose weight they had hot fudge sundaes at Boomers. Why was Rose unable to defend Nancy to Patrick?

Patrick was twenty-four years old, a graduate student, planning to be a history professor. He was tall, thin, fair, and good-looking, though he had a long pale-red birthmark, dribbling like a tear down his temple and his cheek. He apologized for it, but said it was fading, as he got older. When he was forty, it would have faded away. It was not the birthmark that canceled out his good looks, Rose thought. (Something did cancel them out, or at least diminish them, for her; she had to keep reminding herself they were there.) There was something edgy, jumpy, disconcerting, about him. His voice would break under stress—with her, it seemed he was always under stress—he knocked dishes and cups off tables, spilled drinks and bowls of peanuts, like a comedian. He was not a comedian; nothing could be further from his intentions. He came from British Columbia. His family was rich.

He arrived early to pick Rose up, when they were going to the movies. He wouldn't knock, he knew he was early. He sat on the step outside Dr. Henshawe's door. This was in the winter, it was dark out, but there was a little coach lamp beside the door.

"Oh, Rose! Come and look!" called Dr. Henshawe, in her soft, amused voice, and they looked down together from the dark window of the study. "The poor young man," said Dr. Henshawe tenderly. Dr. Henshawe was in her seventies. She was a former English professor, fastidious and lively. She had a lame leg, but a still youthfully, charmingly tilted head, with white braids wound around it.

She called Patrick poor because he was in love, and perhaps also because he was male, doomed to push and blunder. Even from up here he looked stubborn and pitiable, determined and dependent, sitting out there in the cold.

"Guarding the door," Dr. Henshawe said. "Oh, Rose!"

Another time she said disturbingly, "Oh, dear, I'm afraid he is after the wrong girl."

Rose didn't like her saying that. She didn't like her laughing at Patrick. She didn't like Patrick sitting out on the steps that way, either. He was asking to be laughed at. He was the most vulnerable person Rose had ever known, he made himself so, didn't know anything about protecting himself. But he was also full of cruel judgments, he was full of conceit.

"You are a scholar, Rose," Dr. Henshawe would say. "This will interest you." Then she would read aloud something from the paper, or, more likely, something from Canadian Forum or the Atlantic Monthly. Dr. Henshawe had at one time headed the city's school board, she was a founding member of Canada's socialist party. She still sat on committees, wrote letters to the paper, reviewed books. Her father and mother had been medical missionaries; she had been born in China.

**Following
the crowd**

Joyce used the notion of a conformist voice of place to great effect in his 1914 story collection, *Dubliners*. In 'A Mother' we quickly glean the importance that Mrs Kearney places on convention, on appearing normal. Note the ordering of the adjectives by which she judges her choice of husband: 'He was sober, thrifty and pious'. Specificity, of time, numbers, especially monetary numbers, is important too: 'he went to the altar every first Friday'; 'a dowry of one hundred pounds each when they came to the age of twenty-four'. Joyce plays with this reverence of decorum by moving between the language of characters such as Mrs Kearney, so influenced by what is expected of her – 'My good man is packing us off to Skerries' – and a language that transcends this to make ridiculous the petty, unimaginative vision of their lives: 'His conversation ... took place at intervals in his great brown beard.' The orthodox nature of this kind of existence is further ridiculed by the parcelling, in a single sentence, of swathes of life: 'As she was naturally pale and unbending in manner she made few friends at school.'

Dubliners is crowded with characters who, as Joyce himself described his intentions, 'betray the soul of that ... paralysis which many consider a city.' This is evidenced in 'A Mother', as we observe a paralysis of imagination, and parenthood, in the constant shadow of a preeminent church, London, and other conformers.

'A Mother'
from *Dubliners*
James Joyce
1914

Beginning the story with Mr Holohan, then, is significant. We guess, even though he recedes from the narrative, that he will return. His out-of-view presence dogs the seemingly neat order of the story – and Mrs Kearney – as he shambles in the background, ready to upset things. And, incidentally, if you are going to make an investigation of your characters' pockets, here is how to make use of it.

James
Joyce
Dubliners

A Mother

Mr. Holohan, assistant secretary of the Eire Abu Society, had been walking up and down Dublin for nearly a month, with his hands and pockets full of dirty pieces of paper, arranging about the series of concerts. He had a game leg and for this his friends called him Hoppy Holohan. He walked up and down constantly, stood by the hour at street corners arguing the point and made notes; but in the end it was Mrs. Kearney who arranged everything.

Miss Devlin had become Mrs. Kearney out of spite. She had been educated in a high-class convent, where she had learned French and music. As she was naturally pale and unbending in manner she made few friends at school. When she came to the age of marriage she was sent out to many houses, where her playing and ivory manners were much admired. She sat amid the chilly circle of her accomplishments, waiting for some suitor to brave it and offer her a brilliant life. But the young men whom she met were ordinary and she gave them no encouragement, trying to console her romantic desires by eating a great deal of Turkish Delight in secret. However, when she drew near the limit and her friends began to loosen their tongues about her, she silenced them by marrying Mr. Kearney, who was a bootmaker on Ormond Quay.

He was much older than she. His conversation, which was serious, took place at intervals in his great brown beard. After the first year of married life, Mrs. Kearney perceived that such a man would wear better than a romantic person, but she never put her own romantic ideas away. He was sober, thrifty and pious; he went to the altar every first Friday, sometimes with her, oftener by himself. But she never weakened in her religion and was a good wife to him. At some party in a strange house when she lifted her eyebrow ever so slightly he stood up to take his leave and, when his cough troubled him, she put the eider-down quilt over his feet and made a strong rum punch. For his part, he was a model father. By paying a small sum every week into a society, he ensured for both his daughters a dowry of one hundred pounds each when they came to the age of twenty-four. He sent the older daughter, Kathleen, to a good convent, where she learned French and music, and afterward paid her fees at the Academy. Every year in the month of July Mrs. Kearney found occasion to say to some friend:

"My good man is packing us off to Skerries for a few weeks."

If it was not Skerries it was Howth or Greystones.

When the Irish Revival began to be appreciable Mrs. Kearney determined to take advantage of her daughter's name and brought an Irish teacher to the house. Kathleen and her sister sent Irish picture postcards to their friends and these friends sent back other Irish picture postcards. On special Sundays, when Mr. Kearney went with his family to the pro-cathedral, a little crowd of people would assemble after mass at the corner of Cathedral Street. They were all friends of the Kearneys -- musical friends or Nationalist friends; and, when they had played every little counter of gossip, they shook hands with one another all together, laughing at the crossing of so many hands, and said good-bye to one another in Irish. Soon the name of Miss Kathleen Kearney began to be heard often on people's lips. People said that she was very clever at music and a very nice girl and, moreover, that she was a believer in the language movement. Mrs. Kearney was well content at this.

**Going beyond
the everyday**

There is a narrative tension between what normal means to a character and what not normal might mean.

Imagine a line, a straight line, which represents the habitual, everyday existence of a particular character. A life line:

$$\longrightarrow$$

The line is continuous and predictable, until at some point the line ends, in death.

Imagine, as well, other lines – the lives of others – running alongside. Some of these might be in close proximity; others, countless others, will radiate out in increasing degrees of separation.

Each of these lines is a potential narrative through-line of a character's life. The writer can choose where on the line to begin and where to end, and which lines are relevant to each other and, thereby, to the story being told.

You can imagine further that each line is surrounded by its own little box. This box is the character's personal universe – geographically, as well as behaviourally. *This is Jim. We expect to find Jim, in normal times, in this particular place, behaving in this particular way.*

Now imagine Jim's line deviating.

Perhaps it wildly changes course. Or kinks, just for a moment. Or it goes outside the boundaries of its environmental expectations – perhaps to return, perhaps never to return. Or maybe somebody else's line makes contact with it. Perhaps the opening to the narrative is the moment at which a 'normal' line, that is subsequently implied, moves. Think about the last good novel you read. Pick one of the main characters and imagine their normal line. Consider how it veered, how it was touched – and how intrinsic those movements were to your compulsion to continue with the narrative.

The unspoken

In Claire Keegan's short story, 'The Parting Gift', there is a tension in the inference that the main character's normal is about to change, in the mentioning of the suitcase, and New York. This information is embedded within a description of the place she is leaving that is, on the surface at least, bucolic – 'All morning the bantam cocks have crowed' – but with the undertone of this place and the familiar sights and smells of it being connected for her with something else, something darker. The past and the future of the character are in opposition. There is a division between them, which is subtly increased through the story. Look closely, and you will notice recurring symbols of partition, of the open and the closed away:

'She talks through the door'
'the bolt slides back'
'It used to be an open room'
'got the carpenters in and the partition built'

The detail of the key, and 'how much that meant to you at the time' passes by almost unnoticed, buried alongside what we will eventually understand is the most euphemistic description of the whole piece: 'but Eugene put an end to all of that'.

The claustrophobic intensity of the piece is augmented by the use of second-person ('you') narration. The impression is of a muted consciousness, pushing up against the surface – a surface that is always separate from, and incapable of expressing, the real hidden emotion of the main character:

'"It's another fine day." You feel the need for speech.'

The inadequacy of speech is a recurring theme in the story. Dialogue comes in small offerings of phatic nothingness. We can also hear, again, the repetitive voice of the locality: 'It's a fine day for the hay.' The truly momentous thing, though – the secret at the nucleus of the story – is forever unspoken, and it is this tension, between the spoken and the unspoken, that feeds our perception of the main character in every line.

'The Parting Gift' from *Walk the Blue Fields* Claire Keegan 2008

50

When sunlight reaches the foot of the dressing table, you get up and look through the suitcase again. It's hot in New York but it may turn cold in winter. All morning the bantam cocks have crowed. It's not something you will miss. You must dress and wash, polish your shoes. Outside, dew lies on the fields, white and blank as pages. Soon the sun will burn it off. It's a fine day for the hay.

In her bedroom your mother is moving things around, opening and closing doors. You wonder what it will be like for her when you leave. Part of you doesn't care. She talks through the door.

'You'll have a boiled egg?'

'No thanks, Ma.'

'You'll have something?'

'Later on, maybe.'

'I'll put one on for you.'

Downstairs, water spills into the kettle, the bolt slides back. You hear the dogs rush in, the shutters folding. You've always preferred this house in summer: cool feeling in the kitchen, the back door open, scent of the dark wallflowers after rain.

In the bathroom you brush your teeth. The screws in the mirror have rusted, and the glass is cloudy. You look at yourself and know you have failed the Leaving Cert. The last exam was history and you blanked out on the dates. You confused the methods of warfare, the kings. English was worse. You tried to explain that line about the dancer and the dance.

You go back to the bedroom and take out the passport. You look strange in the photograph, lost. The ticket says you will arrive in Kennedy Airport at 12:25, much the same time as you leave. You take one last look around the room: walls papered yellow with roses, high ceiling stained where the slate came off, cord of the electric heater swinging out like a tail from under the bed. It used to be an open room at the top of the stairs but Eugene put an end to all of that, got the carpenters in and the partition built, installed the door. You remember him giving you the key, how much that meant to you at the time.

Downstairs, your mother stands over the gas cooker waiting for the pot to boil. You stand at the door and look out. It hasn't rained for days; the spout that runs down from the yard is little more than a trickle. The scent of hay drifts up from neighbouring fields. As soon as the dew burns it off, the Rudd brothers will be out in the meadow turning the rows, saving it while the weather lasts. With pitchforks they'll gather what the baler leaves behind. Mrs Rudd will bring out the flask, the salad. They will lean against the bales and eat their fill. Laughter will carry up the avenue, clear, like birdcall over water.

'It's another fine day.' You feel the need for speech.

Your mother makes some animal sound in her throat. You turn to look at her. She wipes her eyes with the back of her hand. She's never made any allowance for tears.

'Is Eugene up?' she says.

'I don't know. I didn't hear him.'

'I'll go and wake him.'

It's going on for six. Still an hour before you leave. The saucepan boils over and you go to lower the flame. Inside three eggs knock against each other. One is cracked, a ribbon streaming white. You turn down the gas. You don't like yours soft.

Where do characters come from in the first place?

In all likelihood, the wellspring of your idea, however undefined, is connected somehow to real people. Perhaps your inspiration was a moment in history, an anecdote, a philosophical or political prompt... Whatever it was, real life is usually in the mix somewhere. And not just in the idea itself, but prior to that. Without the experience of interacting with and observing real people, a writer would not be able to create fictional characters.

Characters are a product of the author's total human experience. In that sense, no character in fiction is completely 'made up'.

So don't worry that you should only do one or the other – create an entirely fictitious character, or derive a character from a real person. To varying degrees, all fiction naturally does both.

I have come across many writers who feel hampered by the awareness that they are writing a character based on a real person. If you are too, think about what it is that is inhibiting you – if there is a moral, or a social issue, for instance; or if the knowledge of the real is shrinking the scope of the fictional potential – and deal with it. This might involve telling the person. Or it might involve changing your idea. Remember, too, that even if directly inspired by a real person, the character does not have to be an exact replication. You are writing fiction, not biography. And the reader (yes, this point again) is not fussed about the source material; the reader is interested only in what is there on the page.

**Is this all that
life is?**

For Carver, 'a little autobiography and a lot of imagination are best'. Carver did spend time in a drying-out facility himself, and most of his stories reference a real world that he experienced – factory work, bankruptcy, heavy drinking. He used this experience to give his stories a fierce authenticity while at the same time keeping himself out of the narratives sufficiently that all we focus on are the characters. Story after story, a pattern repeats itself in the struggle of these characters' lives. Mundanity weighs heavily, shot through with moments of deep sadness, and a questioning of the point of it all. 'What's to say?', the narrator of 'Where I'm Calling From' asks, although it turns out he has plenty to say: a paean to the humdrum of life, and doing the best you can. Always there is this discord between the repetitive make-do of day-to-day existing, and a profound, out-of-reach happiness, an answer, somewhere.

In the first person this discord is heightened, the colloquial voice seeming to talk, not to us, but to himself: 'But so what?' The narrator, at first, speaks little about himself. He tells other people's stories, first Tiny's, then J.P.'s. His supposed reason for doing so is that his own story is not worth talking about; it is unchanging. This is the existential discontent that underpins so many of the stories in this collection: that 'normal' is just this – work, poverty, drink, boredom, the TV – and it can never change.

'Where I'm
Calling From'
from *Cathedral*
Raymond Carver
1981

And yet, very often it is the ephemeral action of making contact with another person's life – the 'normal' lines touching: in this story a kiss from J.P's wife; in another, holding a blind man's hand to draw a cathedral – that makes the character fleetingly aware of the overwhelming potential of existence, if not, for most of them, of how to fulfil it.

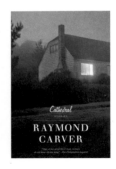

WHERE I'M
CALLING FROM

J.P. and I are on the front porch at Frank Martin's drying-out facility. Like the rest of us at Frank Martin's, J.P. is first and foremost a drunk. But he's also a chimney sweep. It's his first time here, and he's scared. I've been here once before. What's to say? I'm back. J.P.'s real name is Joe Penny, but he says I should call him J.P. He's about thirty years old. Younger than I am. Not much younger, but a little. He's telling me how he decided to go into his line of work, and he wants to use his hands when he talks. But his hands tremble. I mean, they won't keep still. "This has never happened to me before," he says. He means the trembling. I tell him I sympathize. I tell him the shakes will idle down. And they will. But it takes time.

We've only been in here a couple of days. We're not out of the woods yet. J.P. has these shakes, and every so often a nerve — maybe it isn't a nerve, but it's something — begins to jerk in my shoulder. Sometimes it's at the side of my neck. When this happens, my mouth dries up.

It's an effort just to swallow then. I know something's about to happen and I want to head it off. I want to hide from it, that's what I want to do. Just close my eyes and let it pass by, let it take the next man. J.P. can wait a minute.

I saw a seizure yesterday morning. A guy they call Tiny. A big fat guy, an electrician from Santa Rosa. They said he'd been in here for nearly two weeks and that he was over the hump. He was going home in a day or two and would spend New Year's Eve with his wife in front of the TV. On New Year's Eve, Tiny planned to drink hot chocolate and eat cookies. Yesterday morning he seemed just fine when he came down for breakfast. He was letting out with quacking noises, showing some guy how he called ducks right down onto his head. "Blam. Blam," said Tiny, picking off a couple. Tiny's hair was damp and was slicked back along the sides of his head. He'd just come out of the shower. He'd also nicked himself on the chin with his razor. But so what? Just about everybody at Frank Martin's has nicks on his face. It's something that happens. Tiny edged in at the head of the table and began telling about something that had happened on one of his drinking bouts. People at the table laughed and shook their heads as they shoveled up their eggs. Tiny would say something, grin, then look around the table for a sign of recognition. We'd all done things just as bad and crazy, so, sure, that's why we laughed. Tiny had scrambled eggs on his plate, and some biscuits and honey. I was at the table, but I wasn't hungry. I had some coffee in front of me. Suddenly, Tiny wasn't there anymore. He'd gone over in his chair with a big clatter. He was on his back on the floor with his eyes closed, his heels drumming the linoleum. People hollered for Frank Martin. But he was right there. A couple of guys got down on the floor beside Tiny. One of the guys put his fingers inside Tiny's mouth and tried to hold his tongue. Frank Martin yelled, "Everybody stand back!" Then I noticed that the bunch of us were leaning over Tiny, just looking at him, not able to take our eyes off him. 'Give him air!" Frank Martin said. Then he ran into the office and called the ambulance.

Place

There is a concept that you will notice coming up again and again in these chapters: that all of the different features that make up a narrative are inextricably entwined. If you are writing your novel, your short story, thinking, 'I'm going to write a passage on the setting now, then I'll move on to some character backstory, before introducing a plot development...', then the work will likely end up feeling engineered. Engineering of weight and balance comes later. At the instinctive drafting stage, if you are standing outside the text, looking in, analyzing, then you are not sufficiently immersed in the narrative. And, as a consequence, nor will your reader be.

Description of place is an aspect of fiction writing that can tend to get separated from the whole – as a set-up, or a beautiful interlude. It is at its most charged, however, when it melds with plot and character. The meaning of the place is in its relation to the characters that live within it.

The setting of your story is not a framing device.

It is when you view the landscape of the story *through* the filter of the narrative voice that you will find original and relevant ways of describing that landscape. *This* is immersing yourself in the narrative. So, rather than translating your own observations of the physical landscape of the story into whatever is the language of the story, try instead to think *in* that language – the language of the narrative voice.

The landscape of people

What a distinctively imagistic passage this is. Thirty bonfires in the dark, tracing the boundary of the district, lighting up the 'ephemeral caves' of the clouds above them. There is a to-and-fro between the panoramic and the near image, reminding us, reminding the characters, that something greater always surrounds them – reaffirming the bound relationship between the individual and his or her fate. A panorama that is enhanced by the use of the omniscient third person (see page 64), able to pan in and out at will.

> 'It was as if the bonfire makers were standing in some radiant upper storey of the world, detached from and independent of the dark stretches below.'

There is a foreboding sense of the vastness of the landscape: the bonfires 'stood in a dense atmosphere'; 'the mass of shade which denoted the distant landscape'. And of the wildness of the heath, which we intuit (especially if we've read other Hardy novels) is going to have some metaphorical significance. Conformity versus rebellion. Tamed versus free.

The landscape is given human qualities throughout the passage: 'the cheerful blaze', 'winy faces', 'stubborn soil' – driving home the connection between place and people. Even the metaphorical description that is not derived from people is still derived from natural sources: the bonfires were 'like wounds in a black hide'. People, place, nature morphing together to create their own exclusive language: 'The silent bosom of clouds'. Now there's a strand of metaphor that readers of Hardy will be familiar with.

The Return of the Native
Thomas Hardy
1878

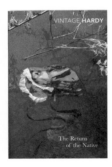

None of its features could be seen now, but the whole made itself felt as a vague stretch of remoteness.

While the men and lads were building the pile, a change took place in the mass of shade which denoted the distant landscape. Red suns and tufts of fire one by one began to arise, flecking the whole country round. They were the bonfires of other parishes and hamlets that were engaged in the same sort of commemoration. Some were distant, and stood in a dense atmosphere, so that bundles of pale strawlike beams radiated around them in the shape of a fan. Some were large and near, glowing scarlet-red from the shade, like wounds in a black hide. Some were Mænades, with winy faces and blown hair. These tinctured the silent bosom of the clouds above them and lit up their ephemeral caves, which seemed thenceforth to become scalding caldrons. Perhaps as many as thirty bonfires could be counted within the whole bounds of the district; and as the hour may be told on a clock-face when the figures themselves are invisible, so did the men recognise the locality of each fire by its angle and direction, though nothing of the scenery could be viewed.

The first tall flame from Rainbarrow sprang into the sky, attracting all eyes that had been fixed on the distant conflagrations back to their own attempt in the same kind. The cheerful blaze streaked the inner surface of the human circle — now increased by other stragglers, male and female — with its own gold livery, and even overlaid the dark turf around with a lively luminiousness, which softened off into obscurity where the barrow rounded downwards out of sight. It showed the barrow to be the segment of a globe, as perfect as on the day when it was thrown up, even the little ditch remaining from which the earth was dug. Not a plough had ever disturbed a grain of that stubborn soil. In the heath's barrenness to the farmer lay its fertility to the historian. There had been no obliteration because there had been no tending.

It was as if the bonfire makers were standing in some radiant upper storey of the world, detached from and independent of the dark stretches below.

15

Everybody reads differently, and some readers will conceive a more imagistically vivid picture of the fictional world than others. All readers, though, will form some kind of perception in their mind, of characters, and of the space that those characters inhabit. Every detail – the silent bosom of clouds, the thirty bonfires – will look different to each reader, for whom every sentence, every word, will come together to bloom into their own imaginative whole. So take care in your choosing of details, because there is great power in them. And don't concern yourself with always trying to create striking and inventive descriptions to dazzle your reader into wonderment at how imaginative you are.

'What an imagination that writer has', a reader might say on finishing a book that has engrossed them. 'No', the writer who truly understands the job and has, for the purpose of my point, menacingly appeared at the reader's side, will reply. 'What an imagination *you* have.' Good writing empowers readers to conjure up a world themselves – and part of a writer's ability to achieve that involves getting out of the way. Dazzling, unless it is vital to the style of the narrative, can strike a false note. It is the creation of detail that is interesting and revealing *inside* the fictional world, the language of the book, that will let the reader occupy it.

The *reader's* imagination is what matters.

Sense the setting

Even though the reader will unconsciously form a picture of the fictional world that is their own, and therefore not exactly the same as the author's perception of it, it is still important that the author forms an impression of what the setting looks like, smells like, feels like.

This will happen naturally, as you immerse yourself in the lives of your characters, cohabiting their senses. You may occasionally hear authors speak about their characters developing a life of their own, which, to my mind, sounds like a psychotic notion. What immersion means, to me, is a totality of empathetic connection, through which you extend your usual reach, feeling the world with the sensual understanding of a new person.

It is a reach, also, that will be extended still further with research. So, when you go to Grimsby to get an idea of the geography of that fishing-community novel, do it with your characters in mind.

Details that would be unextraordinary, missable, if you were passing through simply as yourself, can become, with borrowed eyes and fingertips, completely new.

> Just as you should think in the language of the narrative voice as you write, do the same when researching the place, taking photographs, walking through it.

The intrigue of place

Instead of framing the opening with 'It was a wet rotting October…', *The Carhullan Army* begins with the narrator declaring herself. Character, plot and setting conjoin in an unsettling tone that gives the fiction immediate propulsion – we recognize the world, but begin to understand that there is something changed, something disturbing, about it: 'It was a wet *rotting* October'; the leaves have turned to a 'yellow pulp'. This is not conventional autumnal description; it is an autumn coloured by the perception of the narrator, whose world, we sense, is not conventional, or safe.

There is an abundance of, as yet, unexplained detail about the place. These details make sense to the narrator, but to us they are opaque – they make just enough sense to draw us in, at the same time as being strange enough to stir our intrigue:

'our room in the terrace quarters'
'The bacterial smell of the refinery and fuel plants'
'Each year after the Civil Reorganisation'

And all of these societal details, notice, are infused with description of the setting:

'…and at night and in the mornings something cooler had set in. It was a relief not to wake up sweating under the sheet in our room in the terrace quarters'

The Carhullan Army
Sarah Hall
2007

'The bacterial smell of the refinery and fuel plants *began to disperse at night when the clouds thinned and the heat lifted.*'

'Each year after the Civil Reorganisation *summer's humidity had lasted longer, pushing the colder seasons into a smaller section of the calendar…*'

The effect is cumulative and shocking, as we are carried by the familiar and the unfamiliar in harness, towards the upsetting harmony of character, plot and setting in the line, 'the smog of rape and tar-sand burning off, and all of us packed tightly together like fish in a smoking shed.'

My name is Sister.

This is the name that was given to me three years ago. It is what the others called me. It is what I call myself. Before that, my name was unimportant. I can't remember it being used. I will not answer to it now, or hear myself say it out loud. I will not sign to acknowledge it. It is gone. You will call me Sister.

I was the last woman to go looking for Carhullan.

It was a wet rotting October when I left. In the town the leaves had begun to drop and their yellow pulp lay on the ground. The last belts of thunderstorms and downpours were passing through the Northern region. Summer was on its way out. The atmosphere felt as if it was finally breaking apart, and at night and in the mornings something cooler had set in. It was a relief not to wake up sweating under the sheet in our room in the terrace quarters, coming out of some hot nightmare with milky dampness on my chest. I have always slept better in the winter. It feels like my pulse runs slower then.

This freshness seemed to cleanse the town too. The bacterial smell of the refinery and fuel plants began to disperse at night when the clouds thinned and the heat lifted. Each year after the Civil Reorganisation summer's humidity had lasted longer, pushing the colder seasons into a smaller section of the calendar, surrounding us constantly with the smog of rape and tar-sand burning off, and all of us packed tightly together like fish in a smoking shed.

The change of temperature brought with it a feeling of excitement, an alertness that went beyond nerves or the heightened awareness of the risks I knew I was taking. It was restorative. The cool reminded me of my childhood. Back then the weather had been more distinct, separated.

Point of view

The term *point of view* refers to the narrative voice of a piece of fiction. The originator of its language. 'Who is telling the story?'

There is a rich spectrum of nuance to be experimented with as you find that appropriate mouthpiece. In essence, though, most works of fiction are written from either a *first-person* or a *third-person* point of view.

First person

This is the 'I' voice. The events of the story are narrated by a character who may or may not be directly involved in the story.

> *The moment those little faces began to poke through the bush, I knew that this was not going to end well.*

The text is limited to the thought and description of the narrator – who might well speculate on the thoughts of other characters, but cannot directly access them.

Third person

In third-person narration, access to multiple characters can become freed up, depending on where the narrative falls on the scale between omniscient third person and close third person.

The *omniscient third-person* narrative voice knows everything. It can belong to a character involved in the events of the story, or one who is not involved; or it can be more like a storytelling *presence*, which could in turn feel like a distinctly authorial storytelling presence. Either way, omniscient – or, if you like, distant – narration has the ability to move between different geographical places, and move between and report the hidden thoughts of characters, even, if it wants to, in description of thoughts and events that are happening at the same time.

> *The vehicle stopped. Two men in their late forties, wearing identical suits, shoes and thin maroon ties, got out and walked towards the lump of concrete that sat on the ruptured pavement, while across the city Shep Tammer began, ceremoniously, to undo his trousers in front of Barbara.*

Close third person – sometimes called *free indirect style* – is the language of the narrative in the language of a particular character's mind. In other words: the thought process of the character *is* the text.

> *The sheep was now at the window. Ugly thing. She closed the curtain and sat down on the fold-out banquette as the sound of Peter taking a piss resonated about the caravan. Sweet Lord, she needed a drink.*

Therefore, the narrative – unless the author chooses to hand the mouthpiece over to another character, or nudge the narration along the spectrum towards *omniscient* third person – is limited to the knowledge of that character.

Second person	The thought and description of the narrative belong to a 'you' voice that may not be explicitly identifiable. It might be 'you' the reader; or address another character; or represent the consciousness of the narrator … or it might do all of these things. As such, it can create a slippery and mysterious kind of narration. It is relatively rare as the narrative stance for a novel, largely because it is not easy to sustain in symbiosis with plot and character development (although, for a classic exception, look at *If on a Winter's Night a Traveler* on page 31, the purpose of which is precisely to unstitch our expectations of plot and character development).

> *You think she is looking at you, and you, in turn, watch her close the curtain and sit down so that only the back of her head is visible. A man appears now, coming out of the bathroom. You lower your face once more to the grass.*

First-person plural	Even more infrequently seen than second person, the 'we' voice assumes a communal identity of some kind. Joshua Ferris's *Then We Came to the End* is a notable example.

You might well wonder: Why do I need to know this? And, certainly, knowing the technical terms themselves is not a great deal of use to a fiction writer. However, developing an awareness, as you read other authors' work, of the relationship between the point of view the narrative is written in and the stylistic effect that this brings about *is* useful. The more you think about how the narrative voice of each story and novel you read makes it distinctive, the more potential range you will grow for your own work.

This does not mean that you can simply select a point of view from which to write your project. No writer (I hope) sits at the desk and declares: 'Aha, I shall write in third-person omniscient.' There is a world of stylistic nuance between different points of view (particularly third-person) that defies simplistic grouping together. *The Return of the Native* (page 59) and *The Grass is Singing* (page 89), for instance, both use an omniscient third-person narration, yet they are hardly cut from the same cloth.

As you write your first draft, experiment. If you are writing in first person, try writing a passage in a close third person, and then writing it again more omnisciently, and see how it feels. You never know, it might unlock something. The first few chapters of my first novel, *God's Own Country*, were written in third person, and felt flat. I could not figure out quite why until I gave it a go in first person. At once it became obvious to me that the book was about dialect and place and trustworthiness and various other things that came to me later, but probably wouldn't have done if I had continued pounding away in the point of view that I had decided upon at the outset. Give licence to your instinct. It is the most important tool you have.

> Point of view is not some dry analytical component to impose upon your writing; it is something to explore and have fun with.

Control

Once you have settled on a point of view, don't let it waver unintentionally. Nothing breaks the fictional dream quite like a narrative voice that lurches away from the point of view the reader has settled into.

The narrative voice can be played around with in early drafts, but the finished narrative should not skip or slide between points of view unless there is a particular reason for doing so. One common way of structuring a narrative is to use multiple interlinked points of view. So, a novel might, for example, spend a chapter in close third person with one character, then the next chapter in close third person with a different character. Or use first person for one section, and third person for another (*The Son*, by Philipp Meyer, is a very fine example of such a technique). However you construct your own narrative, though, make sure that if you are going to eschew consistency, you do so with control. Unlike in the following passage:

> *The sheep was now at the window. Ugly thing. She closed the curtain and sat down on the fold-out banquette as the sound of Peter taking a piss resonated about the caravan. Sweet Lord, she needed a drink. She got up again and went to look in the cupboard at Peter's collection of spirit miniatures, huddled together in front of a packet of chocolate biscuits and a half bottle of champagne that Peter was wondering how to present her with that evening before their walk. She took out the gin. On closing the cupboard, the mirrored panel of its door showed her long dark hair and a small birthmark above her left eye.*

You could imagine that she *knows* Peter's secret intention to give her the champagne, and that there is some essential reason for her noting her own appearance. The suspicion, however, is that the author has broken point-of-view consistency unwittingly, in order to give the reader information that the character – and the point of view – would not naturally be party to.

> If you are going to change the mouthpiece, do so purposefully.

Believe me

Whether you want the narrator's recipe for disaster or not, you are being implored to hear it. An implicit deal is struck, in the first-person narrative, between narrator and reader: you will agree to hear this character's story, and you will enter into it with a willingness to believe what you are being told. Inherent in the first-person narrative is the compulsive tension of just how reliable the narrator's account of events is. Do we accept unquestioningly that George is as objectionable as he is being presented here – a man who even as a child believed he was a gift of the gods? The conversational tone is beguiling. So pulled along by it are we that we do not necessarily notice, at first, the subtle implication of a theme being suggested: of sin, of morality. George doesn't just have an arrogant head, he has a 'divinely arrogant head'. His confidence is 'preternatural'. Judgement – personal, moral, societal – lies at the heart of this novel. Just look at the title.

There is an intimacy and immediacy to this collusion between narrator and reader. We go straight into a scene of 'Thanksgiving at *their* house', without any set-up of who *they* are, or who *he* is, or what the impending disaster is, or, indeed, who the narrator is. The utility of this, though, is that we enter seamlessly into his or her world, follow him or her (it's a him, incidentally) in and out of the kitchen, hanging on his jokes and judgements: 'horrible', 'talking about himself', 'given far too much attention', 'gave the impression that he knew something'.

It is as if we are being confided to.

May We Be Forgiven
A. M. Holmes
2012

May We Be
Forgiven

A.M. Homes

"May we be forgiven," an incantation, a prayer, the hope that somehow I come out of this alive. Was there ever a time you thought—I am doing this on purpose, I am fucking up and I don't know why.

Do you want my recipe for disaster?

The warning sign: last year, Thanksgiving at their house. Twenty or thirty people were at tables spreading from the dining room into the living room and stopping abruptly at the piano bench. He was at the head of the big table, picking turkey out of his teeth, talking about himself. I kept watching him as I went back and forth carrying plates into the kitchen—the edges of my fingers dipping into unnameable goo—cranberry sauce, sweet potatoes, a cold pearl onion, gristle. With every trip back and forth from the dining room to the kitchen, I hated him more. Every sin of our childhood, beginning with his birth, came back. He entered the world eleven months after me, sickly at first, not enough oxygen along the way, and was given far too much attention. And then, despite what I repeatedly tried to tell him about how horrible he was, he acted as though he believed he was a gift of the gods. They named him George. Geo, he liked to be called, like that was something cool, something scientific, mathematical, analytical. Geode, I called him—like a sedimentary rock. His preternatural confidence, his divinely arrogant head dappled with blond threads of hair lifted high drew the attention of others, gave the impression that he knew something. People solicited his opinions, his participation, while I never saw the charm. By the time we were ten and eleven, he was taller than me, broader, stronger. "You sure he's not the butcher's boy?" my father would ask jokingly. And no one laughed.

I was bringing in heavy plates and platters, casseroles caked with the debris of dinner, and no one noticed that help was needed—not George, not his two children, not his ridiculous friends, who were in fact in his employ, among them a weather girl and assorted spare anchormen and -women who sat stiff-backed and hair-sprayed like Ken and Barbie, not my Chinese-American wife, Claire, who hated turkey and never failed to remind us that her family used to celebrate with roast duck and sticky rice. George's wife, Jane, had been at it all day, cooking and cleaning, serving, and now scraping bones and slop into a giant trash bin.

**The benefits
of detachment**

The classic mode of the Victorian novel, omniscient third-person point of view has the effect, from *Bleak House*'s first line, of staging the narrative. The scene is constructed before our eyes. Sentences, at first short, sharpened by the omission of verbs, lengthen and rise towards the surprising aside of the Megalosaurus. The atmosphere is thick with a narrative voice that knows everything – everything that is happening now, that has happened before and that is going to happen, everywhere.

This voice is pointedly detached from the events and characters in the novel, yet it is far from neutral. The language is coloured by the narrative voice's complete ownership of the story. Opinion and authority pervade the text. Temple Bar is not simply an obstruction; it is 'that leaden-headed old obstruction'. There is rhetorical display (the word fog is used sixteen times); there are bracketed asides; and there is the explicit metaphorical connection of mud and fog with an intractable law suit.

The novel begins with one seated individual, the Lord Chancellor – then zooms out over the London streets, down the river to the Essex marshes, and simultaneously the Kentish heights, into shipyards, onto boats; there is supple movement too between characters: from the Lord Chancellor to the 'tens of thousands of…foot passengers' (via a Megalosaurus) to horses, 'Greenwich pensioners', the 'wrathful skipper' and the body parts of the 'shivering little 'prentice boy' – before, eventually, the narrative zooms back in on the Lord Chancellor, still at work.

Bleak House
Charles Dickens
1853

Omniscient third-person narration can move swiftly, easily, between places and people, and in so doing is capable (as was Dickens's way) of creating a cast of hundreds. This is made possible – in contrast to, and accented by, this novel's part-time switch to first-person – because the description is done from outside of the characters. What results, in the third-person portion of *Bleak House*, is the portrait not of an individual, but of a city.

CHAPTER I

IN CHANCERY

London. Michaelmas term lately over, and the Lord Chancellor sitting in Lincoln's Inn Hall. Implacable November weather. As much mud in the streets as if the waters had but newly retired from the face of the earth, and it would not be wonderful to meet a Megalosaurus, forty feet long or so, waddling like an elephantine lizard up Holborn Hill. Smoke lowering down from chimney-pots, making a soft black drizzle, with flakes of soot in it as big as full-grown snowflakes—gone into mourning, one might imagine, for the death of the sun. Dogs, undistinguishable in mire. Horses, scarcely better; splashed to their very blinkers. Foot passengers, jostling one another's umbrellas in a general infection of ill temper, and losing their foot-hold at street-corners, where tens of thousands of other foot passengers have been slipping and sliding since the day broke (if this day ever broke), adding new deposits to the crust upon crust of mud, sticking at those points tenaciously to the pavement, and accumulating at compound interest.

Fog everywhere. Fog up the river, where it flows among green aits and meadows; fog down the river, where it rolls defiled among the tiers of shipping and the waterside pollutions of a great (and dirty) city. Fog on the Essex marshes, fog on the Kentish heights. Fog creeping into the cabooses of collier-brigs; fog lying out on the yards and hovering in the rigging of great ships; fog drooping on the gunwales of barges and small boats. Fog in the eyes and throats of ancient Greenwich pensioners, wheezing by the firesides of their wards; fog in the stem and bowl of the afternoon pipe of the wrathful skipper, down in his close cabin; fog cruelly pinching the toes and fingers of his shivering little 'prentice boy on deck. Chance people on the bridges peeping over the parapets into a nether sky of fog, with fog all round them, as if they were up in a balloon and hanging in the misty clouds.

Gas looming through the fog in divers places in the streets, much as the sun may, from the spongey fields, be seen to loom by husbandman and ploughboy. Most of the shops lighted two hours before their time—as the gas seems to know, for it has a haggard and unwilling look.

The raw afternoon is rawest, and the dense fog is densest, and the muddy streets are muddiest near that leaden-headed old obstruction, appropriate ornament for the threshold of a leaden-headed old corporation, Temple Bar. And hard by Temple Bar, in Lincoln's Inn Hall, at the very heart of the fog, sits the Lord High Chancellor in his High Court of Chancery.

**Getting inside
the character's
head**

Unlike the last extract, here all of the narrative emanates from *inside* the main character's mind. In this sense, close third person (and this is very close) is more akin to first person than to omniscient third-person narration. Rather than the narrative directing the character, the character directs the narrative.

So, because the narrative is rooted inside the consciousness of a person, it meanders, because that is what people's thoughts do: '...yer mind just drifted, away into anything, ye didnt even know, just drifting...'. It is effectively – a regular attribute of Kelman's fiction – a stream of consciousness. Notice as well the treatment of dialogue. It is not kept distinct from the rest of the text, as omniscient third person normally would do, but instead is brought close to it so that the two rub noses:

> '...but it was difficult, difficult, just like
> Dad nudged him. You sleeping?
> No.'

Leaving out any punctuation after 'just like' gives us a very real appreciation of how Murdo's dad's words have interrupted his thoughts, and the omission of speech marks also brings us closer to the spontaneity and muddle that real speech often is, and which the standardized presentation of literature can make appear controlled.

The language slides easily into second person, does away with conventional usage of grammar, and uses colloquial expression – all for a more accurate representation of a consciousness than we would get from the structured form of properly punctuated text:

> 'Dad hadnt noticed. The lassies too, ye couldnt help noticing them...'

If not for the few pronouns and the naming of Murdo, this piece could work, technically, in first person. But try swapping them into first person. The narrative loses something of its sap. It becomes more conventional. There is something about the rendering of this text in close third person that defies propriety, and makes it human, alive.

Dirt Road
James Kelman
2016

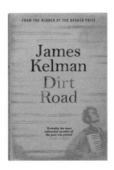

FROM THE WINNER OF THE BOOKER PRIZE

James
Kelman
Dirt
Road

Probably the most
influential novelist of
the post-war period

He hadn't been staring, but there was no point making a fuss. How long since they left home? Ages. Hours and hours. Maybe they could sleep on the bus. Imagine big comfy seats and just lying back, like really comfortable and just closing yer eyes. But if the bus was late what then?

They found space on a bench. Soon Dad had his book out and was reading. Murdo could have brought one. He didnt think of it. Because he didnt know he was going to need it. What did it matter anyway, it was too late; too late for that and too late for this, this and that and that and this, just stupidity, when did that ever happen, forgetting the phone, where was his head, that was the question, all over the place.

Across the side of the hall the police had stopped a guy and were getting him to open his bag. They searched inside, probably for dope. The guy's clothes were out in full view, socks and stuff, underwear. He stood with his head bowed staring at the floor. It wasnt nice.

Dad hadnt noticed. The lassies too, ye couldnt help noticing them; one with bare legs and a short short skirt, quite skinny, and guys staring and she was just like standing there.

Better not thinking about stuff. Music would have helped. A nightmare without it. There was a new system he fancied but it was impossible because of money. Everything was money. It tied in with useless old phones and headsets that dont work. Dad said read a magazine. Okay but ye still heard people talk. Murdo did but Dad didnt. Dad was oblivious to everything. Murdo needed music. So if people talk ye dont hear it, ye dont piece it together. It didnt matter when or where, yer mind just drifted, away into anything, ye didnt even know, just drifting, thinking without thinking, making his mind go in a different way, just to like go cold, make it go cold, but it was difficult, difficult, just like

Dad nudged him. You sleeping?

No.

I could have been away with all the luggage; even your rucksack, I could have lifted it off yer shoulders. I could have stolen everything.

Dad I wasnt sleeping.

Ye were.

I wasn't

Yer eyes were shut.

I was counting to ten and opening them.

Dad sighed. Ye're too trusting. Look after yer things is all I'm saying. There's thieves everywhere.

Language

Should a fiction writer's treatment of language be materially different to that of a non-fiction writer, or a poet?

Fundamentally, no. We are all dealing with words. With the skill and the pleasure of generating meaning out of choosing which words to use, and how to put them together. Sentences in a work of prose fiction are not simple vehicles whose function is merely to carry the next chunk of plot information.

Different arrangements of a sentence – which denotes, on the surface, some explicit piece of information – will have different emotive, imaginative effects on the reader. The placement of a comma. The selection of words. The number of words. The placing and pacing of the sentence within the context of the sentences around it. All will have a minute effect on the reader's perception of a text, whether they are aware of it or not.

Every word of the text carries meaning.

We are schooled to believe that this is poetry's job, this layering of denotative and connotative meaning within words – which often results in the feeling that reading poetry is about detecting secret information, knowable only to the poet and to clever clogs. But poetry does not exist on a different plane from prose. Any line on a page, whatever the form, is layered with different kinds of meaning, both overt and latent.

So play around with your sentences. Take pleasure in words. The more you do, the more your reader will.

Language, used word by word, sentence by sentence in a way that is unique to your own narrative, will hatch a bespoke style of writing. There is no such thing as a pre-set style, just as there is no such thing as a pre-set character.

Of course, there are styles and characters that are reminiscent of others – but really there are as many styles as there are stories, because the linguistic DNA of every narrative in existence is matchless, a snowflake of its own language.

No two narratives are stylistically identical.

This, to me, is also true of different texts written by the same author. Yes, you might well be able to flick through this book and recognize the writing of Raymond Carver, James Kelman, Zadie Smith or Saul Bellow (whose writing is distinctive enough to have its own adjective – Bellovian), but, however recognizable the extracts might be, the innovative chemistry of style and content in each case will always result in something new.

The word 'voice' often gets bandied around when people talk about writing fiction. You must 'find your voice', you might hear, if you want to be an author. I would say, rather, that the individual narrative you are writing should be found a voice – a language of its own. One that may well be very different from your last short story, your next novel. Not only is this a less reductive way of thinking about the originality of each text, it also, let's be honest, makes for considerably less pressure on you.

Joyride

In this extract, language is souped up into a style that is frenzied, inventive, restless. The atmosphere of the city is conveyed by a chaos of sentences that at first appear to bustle together in disorder, but in fact, on closer reading, are in tight harmony.

The kinetic energy of the passage gives the feeling of a New York taxi ride, heightened further by embedding within it the flashback to another journey. Read out loud that sentence about flying, the one beginning: 'They flew through angry spinning snow clouds...'. Listen to the rhythm of it and imagine yourself on a plane, looking out of the window, your view of the earth below punctuated by fast-moving clouds.

The style of this piece marries adroitly with its content, sometimes within an individual sentence and also, more generally, with the character of Herzog himself. At times, he appears to be the originator of the text's thoughts and observations ('horrible! He had to get out to the seashore where he could breathe. He ought to have booked a flight.'), yet there is too much linguistic suppleness and poetry for us to believe that some other narrative impulse is not at work here, too. The resulting effect is a peculiar, crazed control. The two modes bounce off each other. Without the control, this would read clumsily (see Point of View, page 64). Here, though, style and content work together to great effect: Herzog is deliberately not in full control of the narrative, because he is not in full control of his own mind.

Herzog
Saul Bellow
1964

It sounded as though cloth were being torn, not sewn. The street was plunged, drowned in these waves of thunder. Through it a Negro pushed a wagon of ladies' coats. He had a beautiful beard and blew a gilt toy trumpet. You couldn't hear him.

Then the traffic opened and the cab rattled in low gear and jerked into second. "For Christ's sake, let's make time," the driver said. They made a sweeping turn into Park Avenue and Herzog clutched the broken window handle. It wouldn't open. But if it opened dust would pour in. They were demolishing and raising buildings. The Avenue was filled with concrete-mixing trucks, smells of wet sand and powdery gray cement. Crashing, stamping pile-driving below, and, higher, structural steel, interminably and hungrily going up into the cooler, more delicate blue. Orange beams hung from the cranes like straws. But down in the street where the buses were spurting the poisonous exhaust of cheap fuel, and the cars were crammed together, it was stifling, grinding, the racket of machinery and the desperately purposeful crowds — horrible! He had to get out to the seashore where he could breathe. He ought to have booked a flight. But he had had enough of planes last winter, especially on the Polish airline. The machines were old. He took off from Warsaw airport in the front seat of a two-engine LOT plane, bracing his feet on the bulkhead before him and holding his hat. There were no seat belts. The wings were dented, the cowls scorched. There were mail pouches and crates sliding behind. They flew through angry spinning snow clouds over white Polish forests, fields, pits, factories, rivers dogging their banks, in, out, in, and a terrain of white and brown diagrams.

Anyway, a holiday should begin with a train ride, as it had when he was a kid in Montreal. The whole family took the streetcar to the Grand Trunk Station with a basket (frail, splintering wood) of pears, overripe, a bargain bought by Jonah Herzog at the Rachel Street Market, the fruit spotty, ready for wasps, just about to decay, but marvellously fragrant. And inside the train on the worn green bristle of the seats, Father Herzog sat peeling the fruit with his Russian pearl-handled knife.

Perfect pitch

It takes a matter of seconds to read a line, and rarely will a reader pause to deliberate over every word. Nonetheless, in the microspace between each word in a sentence, our minds are still at work, harvesting meaning. After every word, a subconscious expectation of the next word, the next breath of punctuation, is already forming, and there is a compressed subliminal power for the writer in that tiny pause; a potential gratification for your readers when the next word – without knocking them off course – lifts them slightly above that expectation. It is the feeling in your stomach of listening to a beautifully orchestrated piece of music, or driving over a hump in the road.

When the linguistic style of a piece of writing is perfectly in tune with the story being told, we don't simply process lines of information. Our whole being is at work, absorbing, feeling the words. Look again at the passage from *Herzog*. Read this sentence aloud:

'Crashing, stamping pile-driving below, and higher, structural steel, interminably and hungrily going up into the cooler, more delicate blue.'

Here, the rhythm of the sentence is used to replicate its sense. A tiny oasis of calm is hidden amidst the cacophony. Notice how the omission of a comma between 'stamping' and 'pile-driving' gives pile-driving force to the second word. Listen to how the sentence climbs, scaffolded by commas, as the building framework climbs, reaching and stretching until the release of the final comma, the serene momentary glimpse of sky.

The instinctive spark

For the writer, just as much as for the reader, a subconscious energy is at work in the diffusion of a line's meaning. Behind your brain's routine processing of thoughts, and the turning of those thoughts into language, lies an ability to perceive and articulate the world in different ways. You might think, 'Not me, my brain doesn't work like that', but it can and does work like that. Anybody who has learned a foreign language to fluency will recognize this: that a different store of words, with a different mechanism for using them, gives you a new grasp on what is around you. In the writing of fiction, this is the idea I've mentioned already about thinking *in* the language of the narrative, which will let you tap into resources that your everyday descriptive faculties would ignore.

The first draft should encourage an instinctive spark.

I would guess that the 'Crashing, stamping...' sentence from *Herzog* derived from the author's instinctive spark once he was tuned in to the narrative style, the point of view, the character, but that the tailoring of the sentence – its commas, its verb and adverb management – came later.

Accept that some days this spark will happen, other days it will not, but that if you create and maintain the right conditions for it happening, then it will come. And these conditions, at their most basic, are:

Not stewing over getting the line 'right' first time.

Thinking in the narrative voice – its lexicon, its rhythm, its imagery...

Taking the attitude that the development of a narrative style is as much about learning a language as it is about utilizing a language.

You need only observe schoolchildren to understand that a person can be more open-minded and inventive while *learning* than while exercising that learned knowledge.

**Boisterous
lyricism**

Peter Carey is a writer whose novels and short stories tend
to be stylistically different each time. The 'voice' of *True History
of the Kelly Gang* is not the author's; it is unequivocally the
narrator's. In choosing to write a work of fiction about the
mythologized real-life Ned Kelly, a boisterously lyrical language
has been conceived that belongs to an imagined version of that
individual – and it serves to characterize him on every line.

The description is idiosyncratic: 'the shadows of the wattle
was gluey with men's blood', 'my skin were sour with death'.
Non-standard grammar ('We lads come down'), punctuation
('A friend arrived I will not say his name but thank God he
didnt come a day early…') and idiomatic expression ('that
dream were gone to smash') give a fraught pace and vernacular
music to the storytelling. This is the language of Ned,
augmented by the language of the common man and woman
– the Irish convicts banished to Australia – into a linguistic
possession of the text that extends to a claim of truth. Take note
of the title. Note, too, the form of the narrative – a letter from
Ned to his daughter: 'This history is for you and will contain
no single lie may I burn in Hell if I speak false.'

This is what really happened, the content of the novel,
buttressed by its style, is saying. Don't trust the standardizing
narrative of the authorities, the history books. Trust me.

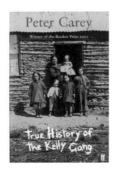

*True History
of the Kelly Gang*
Peter Carey
2000

He were continually breaking off his narrative for he seemed to be suffering very much and who could bear to look upon him so? Not wanting him to linger alone in such agony I quietly reloaded my gun.

He wished to talk about his little boy again weeping frankly at how he missed him every minute of every day.

I then said soon he would be with him.

Sgt Kennedy look up at me sharply. You have shed blood enough said he.

I fired and he died instantly without a groan.

On this day of horror when the shadows of the wattle was gluey with men's blood I could not imagine what wonder might still lie before me. We lads come down across German's Creek into Bullock Creek driving the police horses before us we now had 4 rifles & 4 Webleys and Joe rode with the Spencer slung across his back. As for me my skin were sour with death.

A friend arrived I will not say his name but thank God he didnt come a day early or else he would of been branded a member of the so called KELLY GANG. He and I had wanted no more than land a hearth to sit by in the night but he seen us in possession of the police horses and knew that dream were gone to smash.

The rain begun sprinkling on the dry earth I wished it could wash away my sin but it come on the cold breath of the Southern Ocean there were no forgiveness there. I told my friend I hoped he would get some good grass from this rain he gave me a folded wad of banknotes having sold his stallion for me I asked would he take the money to Mary Hearn.

Harry Power led me to that hut when I were no older than Steve or Dan. This here is Bullock Creek said he it won't never betray you. But it were a dead blind place I knew that at 15 yr. of age it were like a beaten dog cowering in the shadow of the hills.

The invisible author

There is a clean simplicity to this writing, which, although stylistically very different to *True History of the Kelly Gang*, does have one effect in common: the author is invisible. Only the characters matter. We see with perfect clarity 'the fluffy white hair' of the Scottish couple, and feel the 'steady ocean breeze, ideal weather for sightseeing', because there is no authorial fanfare to impede it. Far from being a weakness, the description in this short story benefits from the fact that nothing stands out, on display. You might well not notice on first reading that the word 'bright' is repeated (and will be again, unobtrusively, throughout the story) – just as, later, the presence of monkeys and all the visual and symbolic resonance they will add, is going to build, almost imperceptibly, as the narrative progresses.

Mr Kapasi gently originates the observations in the story: 'Mrs. Das emerged slowly from his bulky white Ambassador, dragging her shaved, largely bare legs across the back seat.' It is his eyes that are viewing her. The style, though, is restrained enough that his judgements, motivation and desires are held back; we are intrigued to know what they are but we are not given them – not yet. The story develops slowly, slyly, under the quiet gaze of this man who is, on one level, a dispassionate tour guide, but on another, as we will find out, is to become emotionally invested in his passengers.

'Interpreter of Maladies' from *Interpreter of Maladies* Jhumpa Lahiri 1999

Interpreter of Maladies

At the tea stall Mr. and Mrs. Das bickered about who should take Tina to the toilet. Eventually Mrs. Das relented when Mr. Das pointed out that he had given the girl her bath the night before. In the rearview mirror Mr. Kapasi watched as Mrs. Das emerged slowly from his bulky white Ambassador, dragging her shaved, largely bare legs across the back seat. She did not hold the little girl's hand as they walked to the rest room.

They were on their way to see the Sun Temple at Konarak. It was a dry, bright Saturday, the mid-July heat tempered by a steady ocean breeze, ideal weather for sightseeing. Ordinarily Mr. Kapasi would not have stopped so soon along the way, but less than five minutes after he'd picked up the family that morning in front of Hotel Sandy Villa, the little girl had complained. The first thing Mr. Kapasi had noticed when he saw Mr. and Mrs. Das, standing with their children under the portico of the hotel, was that they were very young, perhaps not even thirty. In addition to Tina they had two boys, Ronny and Bobby, who appeared very close in age and had teeth covered in a network of flashing silver wires. The family looked Indian but dressed as foreigners did, the children in stiff, brightly colored clothing and caps with translucent visors. Mr. Kapasi was accustomed to foreign tourists; he was assigned to them regularly because he could speak English. Yesterday he had driven an elderly couple from Scotland, both with spotted faces and fluffy white hair so thin it exposed their sunburnt scalps. In comparison, the tanned, youthful faces of Mr. and Mrs. Das were all the more striking. When he'd introduced himself, Mr. Kapasi had pressed his palms together in greeting, but Mr. Das squeezed hands like an American so that Mr. Kapasi felt it in his elbow.

Linguistic style, in 'Interpreter of Maladies', just as in *True History of the Kelly Gang*, and in every other text in this book, is conjoined with what happens in the narrative. But which comes first: style or content? Should a writer think of a storyline, then create a style that best expresses it? Or should the writer first create a way of writing, which will then influence the kind of things that might be written about? Most usually, the process is not so binary as that.

There is no matchmaking procedure; no manual to flick through in order to pick the right pairing. The process is organic. The two form collectively, as the writer tests and sheds various plot directions and linguistic levels so that, at length, they begin to feel in tune. This happens increasingly as the draft progresses, until there comes a point – during the first draft, maybe, or the second; it will be a different point for each project – when you realize that they exist on the page as interdependent bodies of meaning, united.

Style and content develop as one.

When you begin a first draft, neither style nor content will be fully formed – and it is with this first draft that you can experiment, in trying to develop that relationship. The more you take the pressure off yourself to find your own voice, the more flexibility the language and the storyline will have to inform each other, and what will result, eventually, is something unique.

Plot

The plot of a narrative is the pattern of events that occur, set in motion by cause and effect. The simple distinction between plot and story that E. M. Forster described in his book, *Aspects of the Novel*, is a useful one: 'If it is in a story we say: "And then?" If it is in a plot we ask: "Why?"'

Or, you could think of it like dominoes: If the *story* is a long, snaking line of dominoes, then *plot* is what happens when you tip over the first one.

Every writer will approach the creation of plot in their own way. And each work of fiction will have its own plot emphasis, too. Sometimes the idea that you start with will have a plot at its heart; other times not – it might be a character, a philosophical or political propulsion...

I return, though, to my overriding point: you don't need to know the whole thing at the outset, and that includes the plot.

An early plan that you sketch out might give you an inkling of where the first domino might fall; you might also know (or think you know) the ending – or a crucial event somewhere in between. Or you might have none of this. You might simply have an idea of some characters and a vague plan that still looks like nonsense.

Whatever you do have, as you set out on the first draft, you won't hit upon your plot off the page. You will find your plot by writing. The tightening and ordering of it can come later, once you know what it is.

There are numerous theories about basic plots, and how many of them there are. An interesting recent study was conducted by researchers at the University of Vermont, who used a computer program to analyze metadata from 1,327 stories.[1] They found that there are six prominent emotional arcs to a fictional narrative:

> Rags to riches: *Rise*
> Tragedy, or riches to rags: *Fall*
> Man in a hole: *Fall – Rise*
> Icarus: *Rise – Fall*
> Cinderella: *Rise – Fall – Rise*
> Oedipus: *Fall – Rise – Fall*

You can have some fun trying to place different narratives that you have read into these slots. But not your own. Your work of fiction, until it is completed, is limitless, singular. It is not going to help you to imagine Cinderella at your shoulder.

You may well, as you draft, become aware that you are writing something that potentially falls into a certain category, although I would not recommend dwelling on that realization. If you are going to dwell on something, dwell on your characters.

1   Andrew J. Reagan, Lewis Mitchell, Dilan Kiley, Christopher M. Danforth and Peter Sheridan Dodds, *The Emotional Arcs of Stories Are Dominated by Six Basic Shapes*. University of Vermont, Burlington, USA. Published online 4 November 2016.

The collective

A more useful way of looking at plot is to view it as the realization of all the other elements of the work of fiction: character, place, dialogue, language, point of view... None of these stand alone; they are part of a whole – and what you will observe in all of the extracts in this book is that it is only as a collective that they give life to the fiction.

When a full-blooded character behaves in such a way that it causes something to happen in the narrative, think of that moment as a plot point. Usually, as you draft, you might be able to envisage one, or two, potential plot points coming up, and it may well be that you find yourself with the option of going in several different directions. Don't think of this as being in a labyrinth with a choice of doors and if you pick the wrong one then you are screwed.

Even if you revise the shape and the scenes later, the material will still be valuable, because if you have been concentrating on your characters rather than the superstructure of plot, then the general direction of the narrative will probably be the right one.

And remember, again, that you don't have to get it right first time. If the structure, on reading back, doesn't feel coherent, then you will change it.

> If your characters are developed enough that you understand their world and their motivations, then no plot turn is a wrong turn.

The tragedy of ABC

One of the most recognizable plot shapes is the ABC (or 'moral') plot, in which there is a causal thread between A (the entry point to the narrative) and B (some event, or events, brought about by the actions of characters), which in turn causes a reactive behaviour that culminates in C (the denouement). It is also common for a story or novel to open with B or C – sometimes in the form of a prologue – before starting again at A, having set up the intrigue of a promised drama further down the line.

In *The Grass is Singing* we open with C, but what is noteworthy is that Lessing gives us the full thump of the ending up front. Yes, this opening sets up the intrigue of how things might have reached this state, and what the motives of the houseboy were, if indeed he was guilty, but there is no escaping the fact that we know on the first page that the novel's main protagonist will die.

Inescapability, though, is the throb of this novel. Our knowledge of Mary's death induces the tragic inevitability – private, public – that weighs upon every page, and thrusts to the fore the full political vigour of the narrative. And it is, naturally, the storytelling collective that charges the plot. Observe the effect of the omniscient third-person narration, how the events of the novel are peppered at every turn with the invasive judgement of the narrative voice:

The Grass is Singing
Doris Lessing
1950

'When natives steal, murder or rape, that is the feeling white people have.'

I

Murder Mystery
By Special Correspondent

Mary Turner, wife of Richard Turner, a farmer at Ngesi, was found murdered on the front verandah of their homestead yesterday morning. The houseboy, who has been arrested, has confessed to the crime. No motive has been discovered.

It is thought he was in search of valuables.

The newspaper did not say much. People all over the country must have glanced at the paragraph with its sensational heading and felt a little spurt of anger mingled with what was almost satisfaction, as if some belief had been confirmed, as if something had happened which could only have been expected. When natives steal, murder or rape, that is the feeling white people have.

And then they turned the page to something else.

But the people in 'the district' who knew the Turners, either by sight, or from gossiping about them for so many years, did not turn the page so quickly. Many must have snipped out the paragraph, put it among old letters, or between the pages of a book, keeping it perhaps as an omen or a warning, glancing at the yellowing piece of paper with closed, secretive faces. For they did not discuss the murder; that was the most extraordinary thing about it. It was as if they had a sixth sense which told them everything there was to be known, although the three people in a position to explain the facts said nothing. The murder was simply not discussed. 'A bad business,' someone would remark; and the faces of the people round about would put on that reserved and guarded look. 'A very bad business,' came the reply — and that was the end of it. There was, it seemed, a tacit agreement that the Turner case should not be given undue publicity by gossip.

The short story and the novel – does the plot thicken?

A short story, simply because of its length, is unlikely to contain as much plot movement as a novel. Even if there is a distinct plot structure to it (and the shortest short story can sometimes have a more defined plot than the longest novel), it is usually going to be much less complex.

It will often have the atmosphere of a moment in time, in history, which may not resolve, and instead leave the narrative tension in the air.

Even as I write this, inevitably I am thinking of examples that contradict me. But I do believe that, in general, the short story tends to have less reliance on plot. Personally, my favourite short stories are the exquisitely suggestive ones – those that don't let the dream end – rather than the plotbusters.

> A short story is more likely to resonate around a single idea, theme, action, image.

That said, my favourite novels are usually the exquisitely suggestive ones, too. Though, again, I am inclined to contradict myself: *The Grass is Singing* is a novel that moved me a great deal, yet you could hardly describe it as suggestive. It begins by showing you how the dream ends.

**Sometimes
the end is in
the beginning**

The placement of C at the beginning of *The Grass is Singing* implants the tone of the novel, but in the construction of a piece of fiction the author does not necessarily have to decide on such a structure until an advanced stage of development, even if that means the end of an intended final draft. (As it happens, Lessing's novel was originally two-thirds as long again, and had a different central character, who on redrafting was boiled down to a peripheral role, contained within the reworked opening.)

Sometimes an idea that you have just when you think you've finished can be the thing that unlocks the whole narrative. I've experienced that before, and it is a good feeling. Sometimes it might be somebody else's idea. (A less good, but still good feeling.) You should never stop being open to new stimuli.

Once you have a completed draft, which probably has a wonky through-line, gaps and bloating, *now* you can indulge yourself by buying some big paper and marking out the shape of your plot as it stands. You can do this in whatever way feels suitable to you, and to the particular project. If you want to track the pulse of the plot development, a diagram or graph might be useful, with different plot strands showing you visually how they dovetail, augment or impede each other.

Monitoring the flow

Below is the flow chart (that's what I'm calling it, anyway) that I drew up after completing the first draft of my novel, *A Natural*. If you have written a piece of fiction in which there are multiple protagonists whom the novel zooms in on, it can be useful to mark out the focus flow between characters simply to get an overview of the airtime they are each getting – how much, and when.

Any narrative project that is involved with compound moving parts will benefit from a single-page overview of some kind like this chart. The intricacy and density of the whole is easier to get a sight on from above than from inside.

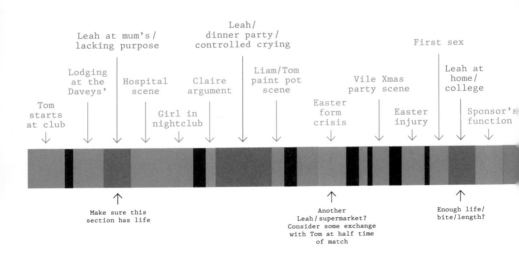

Leah / dinner party / controlled crying

Leah at mum's / lacking purpose

First sex

Lodging at the Daveys'

Hospital scene

Claire argument

Liam/Tom paint pot scene

Vile Xmas party scene

Leah at home / college

Tom starts at club

Girl in nightclub

Easter form crisis

Easter injury

Sponsor's function

Make sure this section has life

Another Leah / supermarket? Consider some exchange with Tom at half time of match

Enough life / bite / length?

Colour codes
of character focus

**Panorama/Broader scene
(23 pages)**
Tom
(131 pages)
**Leah
(33.5 pages)**
Easter
(25 pages)
Liam
(6 pages)

Total
218.5 A4 pages

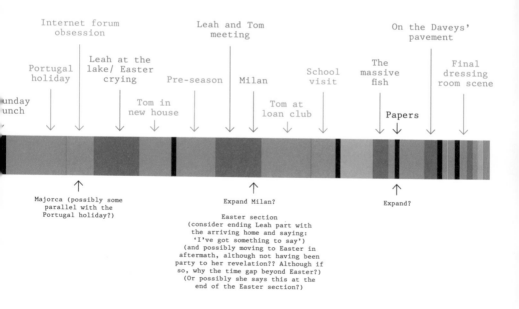

Internet forum
obsession

Leah and Tom
meeting

On the Daveys'
pavement

Portugal
holiday

Leah at the
lake/ Easter
crying

Pre-season

Milan

School
visit

The
massive
fish

Final
dressing
room scene

unday
unch

Tom in
new house

Tom at
loan club

Papers

Majorca (possibly some
parallel with the
Portugal holiday?)

Expand Milan?

Expand?

Easter section
(consider ending Leah part with
the arriving home and saying:
'I've got something to say')
(and possibly moving to Easter in
aftermath, although not having been
party to her revelation?? Although if
so, why the time gap beyond Easter?)
(Or possibly she says this at the
end of the Easter section?)

The anti-plot

Mrs Bridge is situated on the pages like an archipelago, with 117 islands of text – the sum total of her life – through which we travel in gradual, incremental anticipation of the vast nothingness at the end of it.

The genius of the book is that, rather than an ABC plot, we instead have 117 plot points (Connell's later novel, *Mr Bridge*, published ten years later, with the focus on the husband, has 141), which capture perfectly the haphazard, funny, painful, existentially haunting passage of Mrs Bridge's life. She attempts to learn Spanish, and gives up. Her strange son, Douglas, builds an eccentric tower, and loses a model boat race. The Bridges travel to Europe. Mrs Bridge observes Mr Bridge looking in a shop window at a black brassiere with the tips cut off. When her closest friend commits suicide the dramatic import of it is swept aside, even by the chapter heading: 'Tuna Salad'.

The book is full of random episodes of seeming unimportance and, occasionally, an anxious self-doubt about who she is, what she is on the earth for – always unvoiced, to her husband or her children. In so doing, the minute gaze upon this overtly unremarkable housewife in Kansas City, spanning the world wars, makes us start to look deeper, at what humans have made of the world; at ourselves. It is, if you like, the perfect anti-plot.

Mrs Bridge
Evan S. Connell
1959

The next day as they were getting settled on the train for the trip to the Riviera he observed rather dryly that he thought he knew how the Parisian artists kept from starving, but since she had no idea he had bought the painting for her this remark meant nothing, and she replied as she took off her hat that she supposed they must manage some way.

76 • Telegram

A telegram was waiting for them in Monte Carlo. Douglas, knowing the date of his parents' wedding anniversary, sent this message:

MAY I TAKE THE OPPORTUNITY EXTEND FELICITATIONS UPON MEMORABLE OCCASION AND IN BEHALF ENTIRE COMPANY EXPRESS HOPE YOUR CONTINUED SUCCESS.

Mrs Bridge was touched by his thoughtfulness and wrote to him, 'It was awfully sweet to hear from you on our anniversary, but I do think the American Express company must have gotten their messages mixed up....'

[...]

109 • Winter

The snow fell all night. It fell without a sound and covered the frozen ground, and the dead leaves beneath the maple tree, and bowed the limbs of the evergreens, and sifted out of the high, pearl-blue clouds hour after hour. Mrs Bridge was awakened by the immense silence and she lay in her bed listening. She heard the velvet chimes of the clock in the hall, and presently the barking of a dog. She had a feeling that all was not well and she waited in deep expectancy for some further intimation, listening intently, but all she heard before falling asleep was the familiar chiming of the clock.

110 • Tuna Salad

The next morning Lois Montgomery telephoned to say that Grace Barron had committed suicide.

Dialogue

I often hear students say things like: 'My dialogue doesn't feel authentic', or 'I'm no good at dialogue, so I try to avoid putting it in scenes.' Some writers form a block around the idea of writing their characters' speech, as if it is a separate business to everything else that goes into the creation of a piece of fiction. Dialogue, though, is simply another manifestation of character.

> If your dialogue does not feel convincing, it probably means that the characters speaking it are not convincing.

So much of the composition of a work of fiction comes back to this: the more you know about your characters – the intimate details of their history, their relationships, their thoughts, their voice, their physicality, their motivations – the more everything else will come together. We can analyze different aspects of the work separately – the dialogue, the plot, the point of view, and so on – but all of these, fundamentally, are related to, are ingrained in, characterization.

So dialogue, in terms of how it enhances the narrative, is not really any different to the rest of it:

It gives development to the behaviour and motivation of characters.

In so doing it fuels the plot.

The lexicon contained within a character's speech is part of the expression of who that character is; it is itself a form of characterization.

The dialogue will form part, or all, of a scene with which it is therefore amalgamated – integral to the flow, the pacing, the release of information, the interaction of characters.

The words that you choose for your characters to speak are the ones that do those jobs, not an entertaining sidebar to convince the reader that you have an ear for how real people speak.

And the way in which real people speak is usually going to be different to the representation of characters' speech on the page.

Listen in on a real conversation that you are not involved in and note just how much messiness there is. Record it, transcribe it (tell the speakers, I should add, that you are doing so), and then imagine that transcript on the page of a novel. You will probably find at least some of the following:

Overtalking

Repetition (either of what one person has already said, or of what somebody else has already said)

Pauses

Hesitation noises ('ums' and 'ahs')

Bumbling

Discourse markers ('you know', 'like')

Veering off topic

*Hedging ('I **wonder** if you **might** take a look.' 'It was **sort of** impossible.')*

In addition to this padding will be all of the non-verbal features, the smiles and scowls and winks and nods, the physical distance between speakers – all of the body language that cannot be easily transcribed in the speech act. These things, though, are rich territory for the narrative description that might go around and between your dialogue. What is more, if you have created characters that engage the reader, that the reader can form an imaginative appreciation of, then the reader will quite naturally imagine much of this non-verbal behaviour alone, without your guidance.

There is, of course, no rule that says you should never write dialogue that shows all the stumblings and bumblings, the fluff of real speech. To include it would create a quite particular stylistic effect – possibly ridiculousness; possibly, ironically, the revelation of the characters as an artificial construction – which might be exactly what you are after. (Look at *The Driver's Seat* on page 113 for an illustration of both). More often, though, writing dialogue is about making it *seem* true to life. And that is achieved, in large part, by focusing on three main things:

1. Leave the fluff to the reader's imagination	Concentrate on the distilled purpose of showing this conversation, here, at this point in the text. Think about what is needed to do those jobs I mentioned a couple of pages ago: the flow and pacing of the scene; the release of information, of the scene at hand, and the plot as a whole; the interaction of characters.

More often than not, this will mean making the dialogue more concise than a real tract of speech would be. It will mean cutting most, but probably not all, of the fluff of the real. And when you do choose to put the fluff in...

2. Keep the markers of 'realness' subtle	We tend to absorb slang, fillers and repetition with little conscious effort when they come out of a real person's mouth, but on the page these features can become amplified. A real person might well finish every sentence with 'you know', but if a character on the page did it most readers would be likely to find their speech tiresome and distracting, and struggle to escape the perception that the author was trying too hard to make the character appear authentic. It is worth repeating that this is not to say that verbatim speech *cannot* work on the page, but where it does it is almost always in keeping with the creative intention of the whole piece – as James Kelman (see the extract from *Dirt Road* on page 73) manages so adeptly, making the vernacular language of the character form the language of the novel.
3. Make your characters speak differently from each other	Again, subtly. Because this is another thing that can be more pronounced on the page than out of the mouth. It is, however, logical that the way in which each person in the piece of fiction speaks should be consistent with their character. Do they say a little or a lot? What subjects preoccupy them? What vocabulary do they use? Does their register fluctuate – sometimes formal, sometimes informal, depending on whom they are speaking to? Do they speak in tidy, complete sentences, or does their speech sometimes falter, tail off…

| The performance of conversation | There is no one way to present dialogue on the page. This example from *On Beauty* uses conventional punctuation and an array of techniques to exhibit how the words are being spoken. We are shown exactly the performative nature of speech, and what results is a subtle separation of the characters and the storytelling voice. |

Interjections of narrative description occur throughout the conversation ('Kiki laughed in an unhinged way', 'Kiki was vulnerable to compliments concerning her children'). The speech is often tagged as belonging to a particular speaker. This tag also sometimes lets us know, with an adverb, or a verb other than 'said', what the speech might sound like ('began Kiki happily'). Some of the rigging of real speech is shown, in *hesitations* ('…are you…Mrs Kipps or…'), *interruptions* ('and then you and Levi bumping –'), and *accenting* ('I *knew* I was right'). A real conversation between these two women would probably contain even more of these features, but the ones used here have been chosen selectively, to create a sense of the mood, physicality and power dynamic between the two speakers.

The effect of this puppeteering is twofold: humour springs from the awareness of the characters as constructions, while the suppleness of the movement – inside, outside characters' minds, forwards and backwards over time and place – gives the narrative the ability to encompass a cast of many characters, building, as Zadie Smith's novels do so well, a multilayered portrait of a community.

On Beauty
Zadie Smith
2005

Equally, it didn't seem right to wake her. On the porch now and hesitating, Kiki had the momentary fancy of placing the note in the woman's lap and running away. She took another step towards the door; the woman woke.

'Hi, *hi* — I'm sorry, I didn't mean to alarm you — I'm a neighbour here...are you...Mrs Kipps or...'

The woman smiled lazily and looked at Kiki, around Kiki, apparently assessing her bulk, where it began and where it ended. Kiki pulled her cardigan around herself.

'I'm Kiki Belsey.'

Now Mrs Kipps made a jubilant sound of realization, beginning on a reed-thin high note and slowly making its way down the scale. She brought her long hands together slowly like a pair of cymbals.

'Yes, I'm *Jerome's* mother — I think you bumped into my youngest today, Levi? I hope he wasn't rude at all...he can be a little brash sometimes —'

'I *knew* I was right. I *knew* it, you see.'

Kiki laughed in an unhinged way, still concentrating on taking in all the visual information about this much discussed, never before glimpsed entity, Mrs Kipps.

'Isn't it crazy? The coincidence of Jerome, and then you and Levi bumping —'

'No coincidence at all — I knew him by his face the moment I saw him. They're so alive to look at, your sons, so handsome.'

Kiki was vulnerable to compliments concerning her children, but she was also familiar with them. Three brown children of a certain height will attract attention wherever they go. Kiki was used to the glory of it and also the necessity of humility.

'Do you think so? I guess they are — I always think of them still as babies, really, without any —' began Kiki happily, but Mrs Kipps continued over her, unheeding.

'And now this is you,' she said, whistling and reaching out to grab Kiki's hand by the wrist. 'Come here, come down.'

'Oh...OK,' said Kiki. She crouched beside Mrs Kipps's chair.

'But I didn't imagine you like this at all. You are not a *little* woman, are you?'

Going over it later, Kiki could not completely account for her own response to this question. Her gut had its own way of going about things, and she was used to its executive decisions, the feeling of immediate safety some people gave her, and conversely, the nausea others induced.

Behind the scenes of the conversation

In this extract, the characters' speech is immersed inside the narrative and, crucially, inside the narrator's head. There are no speech marks, because the line between truth and untruth, between reality and the narrator's version of reality, is not a clear one in this novel. The character voices this narrative, not an external storyteller. In moments that are heightened by confrontation and violence (of which there are not a few), it becomes increasingly difficult for the reader to know what is actually going on. The narrator is unreliable. He becomes, as the novel advances, more and more deluded.

Even here, early on in the book, it is hard to be entirely sure what, if any, of 'He was always busy with his lessons, working things out. Investigating this and that. That was the kind of Philip' is spoken, and what is inside Francie's head. Is the first part inside his head, then 'That was the kind of Philip' voiced, as if Mrs Nugent has understood the first part? Or is it all voiced? Or none of it?

Narrative description and dialogue bleed together as a stream of consciousness in this novel. And we, the readers, are brought uncomfortably close to it, because the absence of any separation between events, character and storytelling voice confines us. We, like the narrator himself, are trapped inside his head.

The Butcher Boy
Patrick McCabe
1992

It was a nice warm room with an amber glow that reached out to you and beckoned you in. Come on in, it said, so I thought maybe I would but then knock knock and out comes Mrs Nugent. She was a long way now from the rose in her hair all right. Cupid's bow lips! What a joke! She had on a raggy old apron with forget-me-nots scattered all over it and a heart-shaped pocket bulging with clothes pegs.

I had to laugh at the furry boots.

She must have been washing for she had on rubber gloves and was pulling at the fingers. A crinkly arrow appeared over her eyes in the middle of her forehead and she said what do you want. No she said what do *you* want? I could see in the hall. There was a barometer pointing to very hot some barometer that was. They say there's going to be rain Mrs Nugent I said, rubbing my hands together all business. That won't please the farmers. What do you want she said again. Then she said it *again* and I said nothing much just called down to see how Philip is getting on. Philip is very busy with his lessons, she said. I knew he was. He was always busy with his lessons, working things out. Investigating this and that. That was the kind of Philip. That's what I said to Mrs Nugent. Mr Professor, I said, always busy! Nugent said nothing. She was picking at one of the clothes pegs inside her pocket. Well that's the Christmas over now for another year Mrs Nugent I said but she said nothing to that. All over now, I said again, it'll be very quiet now till Patrick's day. Yes, she said.

I suppose you're glad to get it all over with, I said and folded my arms. I smiled. She picked little bits off the inside of her lip and said yes she was. Then she whispered goodbye now and made to close the door but I stuck my foot in the jamb and held it fast.

Sex

It is perhaps symptomatic of Western (and especially British) attitudes towards sex that 'erotic' fiction exists as a separate, giggled-at, genre of writing. There is no subcategory of 'work' novels, or 'eating' novels, is there? Sex, however, is a normal aspect of human existence, too, and the writing of it in any fiction provides an opportunity to delve into the intimate, private lives of characters in a way that is usually less accessible in the real world – where we are more likely to view sex through the warped glass of infantilism, banter or pornography. Make the most of that opportunity. Sexual attraction and encounter is likely to be an important part of your characters' lives, so don't avoid it, and don't go about it sheepishly either.

The reader is not imagining *you*, the author, in bed.

The reader is imagining *your characters* in the bed. As you should be. In fact, it is only when an author lets self-consciousness creep into the writing of sex that a reader will start to be aware of him or her.

We recognize this self-consciousness in the form of cliché, saturated metaphor, stylistic flourish or heavy inference of the act indirectly described.

Sex, like everything else, should be in step with the language of the whole.

But what to do with the body parts?

Do you, in real life, refer to your penis as a member? A manhood? A desire? Do you put your daughter in the bath and remind her to wash her trembling flower?

Perhaps you do – and where in the world you are reading this book will inevitably have a large bearing on this, as different languages, different cultures, treat the anatomization of genitalia very differently – but the important thing for you is to think about how the language of sex fits the style of your piece. We notice immediately when a work of prosaic realism is suddenly lifted in tone and vocabulary for a passage of sexual description. The effect is rarely beneficial.

> You wouldn't have sex wearing a mask of somebody else's face, unless it was for a creative reason. Your writing of sex should keep to the same principle.

The sooner you stop thinking about yourself, the better. Your characters probably do lots of things differently to you: the way they interact and think and speak and joke and dress and argue with broadband providers on the phone. It is only natural, as well, that they have a different kind of sexual experience to your own, so there is no need to treat sex any differently to other facets of characterization. Liberating yourself from your own limited (to one person's) sexual knowledge can only have the effect of liberating your writing.

Partnering fantasy with reality

The rubbing together of contrasting diction in this passage throws off sparks: 'the flames around Joan of Arc at the stake' / 'he entered my butt with the rest of his hand'; 'the metaphoric auto-da-fé' / 'taking a dump'. The language and reference toy with the unexpected, which is entirely in keeping with the style of this novel, and this passage is a good illustration of the oddball, skittish, self-analytical tenor of the whole.

The first-person narrative is addressed to an implied audience, which, as the novel progresses, you could increasingly deduce to be the narrator herself. This lends the novel its air of uncertain dreaminess, as the narrator fumbles for purpose, for an identity. It makes sense that sex might increase that tension between fantasy and reality. So this passage is loaded with surprising sentences sprung between the two positions:

'I was still struggling to dissociate myself into an out-of-body experience when Stephen came, crying out like a dinosaur.'

The narrative flits between a churning consciousness, as the narrator tries to make sense of her relationship with Stephen, with the world, and the sudden opening of her eyes to see that, yikes, this is what's actually happening.

'Look at Stephen! He thinks he's having sex! Smell his hand! It's touching my hair!'

The Wallcreeper
Nell Zink
2014

106

We kissed, but my whatever had not healed. It was hot and dry. (I mean my brain.) I just stood there in a state of mournful passivity while he knelt down and licked me, touching my asshole rhythmically with one finger and petting my thigh in counterpoint. I felt sad. His awkward hands reminded me of the flames around Joan of Arc at the stake. But I knew after we started to have actual sex I would feel better. However, that was before he entered my butt with the rest of his hand followed by his penis and the metaphoric auto-da-fé became a thick one-to-one description of taking a dump.

Now, all my life I had fantasized about being used sexually in every way I could think of on the spur of the respective moment. How naïve I was, I said to myself. In actuality this was like using a bedpan on the kitchen counter. I knew with certainty that "pain" is a euphemism even more namby-pamby than "defilement". Look at Stephen! He thinks he's having sex! Smell his hand! It's touching my hair! I thought, Tiff my friend, we shall modify a curling iron and burn this out of your brain. But I didn't say anything. I acted like in those teen feminist poems where it's date rape if he doesn't read you the Antioch College rules chapter and verse while you're glumly failing to see rainbows. I was still struggling to dissociate myself into an out-of-body experience when Stephen came, crying out like a dinosaur.

I gasped for air, dreading the moment when he would pull out, and thought, Girls are lame.

Originality

There are speaking events aplenty in which people from the book industry – agents, editors – will give advice to writers embarking on their first book. They will invariably say that what they are looking for is something original. An original voice. The result is often that the aspiring writers, on hearing this, go away and contrive works of fiction that are in fact much like what has gone before: the quirky child narrator; the reclusive young female protagonist who holds a secret; the 800-page polyphony.

Strikingly original fiction that is any good never comes from the starting point of an author aiming to write something that is strikingly original. It will have a similar starting point to any good piece of fiction: an idea, from which the author creates a world, and immerses him or herself in it. Originality is about the distinctness of this new world, this dream. When readers enter a dream that they perceive as being new to them, they will likely feel that this is an original narrative – and in this sense *all* fictional narratives, if they are doing the job of fiction (and it's worth remembering here that the word 'novel', as an adjective, means 'interestingly new') are original. Nobody has ever written those words in that combination before, about those characters, in that setting. So, often when we say that something is original, what we really mean is just that it's bloody good.

Ideas, and the form that will communicate those ideas, fuse in the drafting process to become a new entity. Sometimes the result of this hybridization, though new, might bring existing texts to mind; sometimes, a strange virgin creation might emerge. Nobody is going to care either way, though, unless the writing moves them to read it. So a sizeable undertaking of care and craft with regard to all the topics represented by the chapter headings in this book will always be necessary, however fresh the narrative is.

> When we talk about originality, it might be the originality of the storyline, or it might be the originality of form — but if it is truly original, the two go hand in hand.

An original form, used to communicate a conventional story, is often going to appear pretentious. An original story idea, written in a conventional way, will fare better, but will likely end up feeling placeable, safe. Sometimes, as a reader, safe is what we want. A new take on a familiar model, when we don't know what we are getting, but we do know how it will be given to us. For most of us, our reading habits, much as our TV- and film-watching habits, will involve a bit of both: sometimes the thing that is dependable, and sometimes, when we are in the mood, the thing that takes us somewhere we have not been before.

Rejecting realist convention

I imagine that, until you have read more than this single-page opening of *A Girl is a Half-Formed Thing*, this may well look like gobbledygook to you. The deconstruction of language, syntax and rhythm from any recognizable form necessitates a new way of reading to go along with the new way of writing.

One person's experience of being human is not the same as the next person's – so why should writing, which is about characters, who are usually human, be normalized? This novel uses an idea more readily associated with drama: the art of experiencing, as opposed to the art of representation.

Realist convention would probably attempt to wring some careful emotive detail out of the boy's blood seeping through his head bandaging, or from his eye not opening properly. Here, that kind of focus on detail is done away with. The writing cuts straight to the core. It moves so quickly over details that we cannot slot them into any recognizable trope of realism. Time and place are not given. Characters are not named. Descriptions of appearance are rarely given. Dialogue is not constructed in a 'normal' way – it is simply flung in, unpunctuated.

And all of this, whether you like it or not, expresses brutally the speed and the incomprehension of the events of the narrator's life; the way in which she reacts to her brother's brain tumour. The author, Eimear McBride, has described the novel as 'stream of existence', a useful term that, once you give yourself over to what it means as you read the book, urges you to break free from trying to understand the narrative in an orthodox way.

A Girl is a Half-Formed Thing
Eimear McBride
2013

1

For you. You'll soon. You'll give her name. In the stitches of her skin she'll wear your say. Mammy me? Yes you. Bounce the bed, I'd say. I'd say that's what you did. Then lay you down. They cut you round. Wait and hour and day.

Walking up corridors up the stairs. Are you alright? Will you sit, he says. No. I want she says. I want to see my son. Smell from dettol through her skin. Mops diamond floor tiles all as strong. All the burn your eyes out if you had some. Her heart going pat. Going dum dum dum. Don't mind me she's going to your room. See the. Jesus. What have they done? Jesus. Bile for. Tidals burn. Ssssh. All over. Mother. She cries. Oh no. Oh no no no.

I know. The thing wrong. It's a. It is called. Nosebleeds, head aches. Where you can't hold. Fall mugs and dinner plates she says clear up. Ah young he says give the child a break. Fall off swings. Can't or. Grip well. Slipping in the muck. Bang your. Poor head wrapped up white and the blood come through. She feel the sick of that. Little boy head. Shush.

She saw it first when you couldn't open your eye. Don't wink so long wind'll change and you'll stay that way. I'm not Mammy. It's got stuck. She pull it open. Hold it up. I can't it's all fall down.

And now Holy Family on a Saturday night. He is leaning you are sleeping she the chair me whirlabout. Listen in to doctor chat. We done the best we could. There really wasn't much. It's all through his brain like the roots of trees. Sorry. Don't say. That. He's running out I'm afraid. I'm afraid he's running down. You should take him home, enjoy him while you can. He's not. He is. Can't you operate again? We can't. Shush. Something? Chemo then. We'll have a go at that.

**Weirding the
reader out**

Again, though in a very different way, the originality of this
passage comes from its spurning of realist convention. Here
the language and grammar are more familiar – which only
accentuates the oddness of the piece, because we are tricked
into perceiving character and event using our habitual realist
fiction-reading gaze, but then find we cannot fathom what is
going on. It's just too odd.

We are alienated from the character because she behaves,
and is linguistically expressed, in a way that we are unprepared
for. She is not named, and remains 'the customer', even though
we sense her prominence as a protagonist compared to 'the
salesgirl'. The strange opening dramatic event of her tearing
the dress off is suddenly abandoned for a lengthy description
of the dress, then of its commercial lack of success, and then
of the other dresses 'in the back storeroom awaiting the drastic
reductions of next week's sale'. The obfuscating tone produced
by this movement is heightened by the use of present tense
('she is saying') because it takes us even further from the notion
that this is a story with a purpose, constructed from events that
have happened and are noteworthy.

One of the things that makes this writing so unexpected,
and postmodern, is that the kind of character interiority that
realism might give us is completely denied. Instead, through
the omniscient third-person point of view, we view her as a
kind of specimen. Omniscient narration is sometimes described
as being like a camera looking down on events, zooming in,
zooming out. This, then, is CCTV: the unsettling, murky
monofocal image of a character under examination, whose
inner feelings and motives are impossible to know.

The Driver's Seat
Muriel Spark
1970

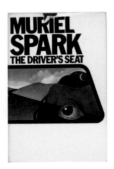

I

'And the material doesn't stain,' the salesgirl says.

'Doesn't stain?'

'It's the new fabric,' the salesgirl says. 'Specially treated. Won't mark. If you spill like a bit of ice cream or a drop of coffee, like, down the front of this dress it won't hold the stain.'

The customer, a young woman, is suddenly tearing at the fastener at the neck, pulling at the zip of the dress. She is saying, 'Get this thing off me. Off me, at once.'

The salesgirl shouts at the customer who, up to now, had been delighted with the bright coloured dress. It is patterned with green and purple squares on a white background, with blue spots within the green squares, cyclamen spots within the purple. This dress has not been a successful line; other dresses in the new stainless fabric have sold, but this, of which three others, identical but for sizes, hang in the back storeroom awaiting the drastic reductions of next week's sale, has been too vivid for most customers' taste. But the customer who now steps speedily out of it, throwing it on the floor with the utmost irritation, had almost smiled with satisfaction when she had tried it on. She had said, 'That's my dress.' The salesgirl had said it needed taking up at the hem.

Information overload

Look at the sheer amount of information contained in that first sentence. We are not able to settle, as our expectations are constantly subverted: the choppiness of tense, the tension induced by multiple stacked clauses, the surprise of the gun, the layers of implicit questions. There would be a natural end to the sentence at 'aimed her own father's gun at her heart', but the sentence runs on, forcing the rhythm uncomfortably into the askew detail of the dining room and the 'three guests', making us juxtapose the two jarring images – the visceral gory shock of upstairs with the quiet politesse of downstairs.

There are only four sentences on this page. If you break each of them down into their comma-separated chunks, you will see that they form a flick book of images. Through the narrator's rhetorical rough-housing of language, some of these images are repeated using the same words ('she stood before the mirror, unbuttoned her blouse, took off her bra'), yanking us forwards and backwards, disorienting us, visually and temporally.

This narrator is a keen student of events, and is also involved in them – begot, in fact, as a result of this opening tragedy. The more he inspects, the more microscopic yet convoluted become his observations, so that we know everything there is to know, and thereby begin to understand that, really, we know nothing – just as the narrator knows nothing – about anybody beyond our own selves.

A Heart So White
Javier Marías
1992

I did not want to know but I have since come to know that one of the girls, when she wasn't a girl anymore and hadn't long been back from her honeymoon, went into the bathroom, stood in front of the mirror, unbuttoned her blouse, took off her bra and aimed her own father's gun at her heart, her father at the time was in the dining room with other members of the family and three guests. When they heard the shot, some five minutes after the girl had left the table, her father didn't get up at once, but stayed there for a few seconds, paralysed, his mouth still full of food, not daring to chew or swallow, far less to spit the food out on to his plate; and when he finally did get up and run to the bathroom, those who followed him noticed that when he discovered the blood-spattered body of his daughter and clutched his head in his hands, he kept passing the mouthful of meat from one cheek to the other, still not knowing what to do with it. He was carrying his napkin in one hand and he didn't let go of it until, after a few moments, he noticed the bra that had been flung into the bidet and he covered it with the one piece of cloth that he had to hand or rather in his hand and which his lips had sullied, as if he were more ashamed of the sight of her underwear than of her fallen, half-naked body with which, until only a short time before, the article of underwear had been in contact: the same body that had been sitting at the table, that had walked down the corridor, that had stood there. Before that, with an automatic gesture, the father had turned off the tap in the basin, the cold tap, which had been turned full on. His daughter must have been crying when she stood before the mirror, unbuttoned her blouse, took off her bra and felt for her heart with the gun, because, as she lay stretched out on the cold floor of the huge bathroom, her eyes were still full of tears, tears no one had noticed during lunch and that could not possibly have welled up once she'd fallen to the floor dead. Contrary to her custom and contrary to the general custom, she hadn't bolted the door, which made her father think (but only briefly and almost without thinking it, as he finally managed to swallow) that perhaps his daughter, while she was crying, had been expecting, wanting someone to open the door and to stop her doing what she'd done, not by force, but by their mere presence, by looking at her naked, living body or placing a hand on her shoulder.

Of course, a work of highly inventive fiction is not going to be to every reader's taste. It will no doubt divide opinion, or not be widely read ... until, that is, its originality becomes celebrated enough that it is aped, followed by other narratives influenced by it. A work that inspires other work is no bad thing – it is a vital thing, in fact, because mould-breaking pieces are the instigators of movements, schools of thought, cultural progression. And fiction is always, at any particular moment in time, pulling in multiple directions simultaneously. It is never a solid homogenous block.

Literature dances to different beats — narratives twisting in and around each other, while being absorbed in their own music.

At this particular moment (which will no doubt feel dated to the reader of this book in a few years' time), thought-provoking new examples of myriad forms are springing up all around us: of autofiction; of linguistic distortion, as in the extract we have just looked at from *A Girl is a Half-Formed Thing*, or Mike McCormack's single-sentence novel, *Solar Bones*; the quick-response novel to a topical issue, such as Ali Smith's *Autumn* or *The Cut*, by Anthony Cartwright – both published in response to Brexit – or *Pussy*, by Howard Jacobson, a quick-fire retort to the Donald Trump presidency.

Without continual invention, literature would become static and die. In busting a norm, you create a new norm, which, in turn, will get bust.

The pages of this book are full of mould-breakers. In addition to Eimear McBride, Muriel Spark and Javier Marías, the writing of Raymond Carver, Lydia Davis, James Kelman, Zadie Smith and James Joyce was all electrifyingly new at one time.

An idea can only be the first of a kind once.

To some, very original works can, over time, come to feel dated, pressed to flatness by the weight of words that have been piled on top of them – though I have to say that, as far as I am concerned, the very best writing always stands alone, whatever comes after it.

'If it sounds like writing,
I rewrite it.'
—Elmore Leonard

Chapter Three

Honing

The ending
Editing
Life, writing

Extract of great writing

Denis Johnson:
Train Dreams

The ending

The ending to your narrative is, like the opening, a seamless part of a whole. The last chapter, last page, last sentence – none of these should be a cherry on the cake. Now really isn't the moment to wake your reader up from the fictional dream in order for you to declare yourself. Or for some other emotion – of relief or sentimentalism – that an author might feel on reaching the end, to invade the work.

Your method, however, will guard you against any inconsistency. Even if the triumphant flush of finishing has coloured the ending in some way, your redrafting and editing will give you the opportunity to recognize and to change it. It might well be the case, in fact, that your first draft lacks an ending altogether.

You do not need to have an ending down until the work is completed.

If you just cannot think how to end it as you are progressing towards what feels like the culmination of your first or second draft, then don't. The further down the line you get with your process, the better you will know your material, and so the better placed you will be to decide how to draw it to a close.

Of course, it will sometimes be the case that the idea of a denouement is bound to the concept itself; maybe the only idea you have is an ending; maybe you realize midway through your first draft that you have unwittingly written the ending already. All of these circumstances are normal, and if you have developed a surety in your method of putting together a piece of fiction, you will be able to deal with the ending, however it comes to you.

But what *kind* of ending should your narrative have? Just as it is not helpful to think in terms of different categories of character, or style or point of view, the same goes for endings, although it is interesting to note certain variations. The main one being the contrast between a short-story ending and a novel ending. A short story always transmits an awareness of its ending, purely because of its length. The reader starts to read probably knowing roughly when he or she will finish it, and for this reason the reader will have a particular hunger, all the way through, for the ending. With a novel, this hunger does not usually develop until the reader is some distance into the book.

Yet the endings to short stories are, not always, but time and again, left open. It suits the short-story form to end the narrative with a sense of characters' lives continuing. It is the feeling that in reading the story we have dipped into an intense moment of something larger.

This is the reason that I, personally, tend to find myself lingering inside the world of a short story, after finishing it, for longer than I do with most novels. The story itself might be shorter, but the imaginative potential of the fictional dream is just as large.

Style, whatever the length of the fiction, will have some bearing on the kind of ending it has. Naturalistic fiction, such as James Kelman's *Dirt Road* (see page 73), can incline towards an open ending, and it is not insignificant, either, that the very close third-person point of view that Kelman regularly uses also suits the open ending. The deeper inside the consciousness of a character the writing is, the more uncontrived it may feel to leave the character alive in the reader's imagination; whereas an omniscient third-person point of view can have a greater capacity to close out, to wrap up. *The Return of the Native* (see page 59), as is typical of the novels of Thomas Hardy, and indeed Victorian novels in general – being predominantly omniscient, and often serialized – closes out in such a way:

'Some believed him, and some believed not; some said that his words were commonplace, others complained of his want of theological doctrine; while others again remarked that it was well enough for a man to take to preaching who could not see to do anything else. But everywhere he was kindly received, for the story of his life had become generally known.'

The ending to your narrative might bring us back in some way to the opening, as we read in *The Grass is Singing* (see page 89). Or it might have an eye on a follow-up (*Wolf Hall*, for instance). Or, as the following example demonstrates, it might link thematically to the fabric of the whole.

Holding off the tub-thumping ending

This final page of *Train Dreams* requires no plot-spoiler alert. This is a novella in which the plot has already been unthreaded. The narrative moves back and forth through time, sometimes with overt flashbacks, but more often, as here, by simply picking up the main character's life at various points, fragmenting his existence into many parts that run alongside each other without ever joining into something definitive. The very choice of form – a novella of about 100 pages – to portray the whole life of a man, during an epic, expansionist period of American history, is a challenge to the assumed supremacy of man's place in nature and in time.

Train Dreams is profoundly concerned with time. The smallness of an individual life in time's vastness; our powerlessness to control it, or to predict the future. The main character, Robert Granier, confuses the chronology of his past. He cannot even be sure what year (or country) he was born in. He is completely without eminence, a nobody. Yet one of the delicacies of the book is that it manages to suggest this without ever belittling the character. Instead, it steeps him in a raw appreciation of the beauty and wonder of the natural and unnatural world around him. Of vast canyons, spirits, even the magnificence of a forest fire that kills his family, and, in this final passage, of a 'counterfeit monster' whose roar begins to take on the symbolic value of all the strangeness of human existence. It is cacophonous, overwhelming. There is a train whistle intermingled. (Trains, themselves symbolic of the breakneck, intrepid, solitary advance of mankind, are everywhere in the book.) He is enthralled by this moment with the wolf-boy. And then, like everything else, it is gone.

Train Dreams
Denis Johnson
2002

They had given their money to preachers who had lifted their hearts and baptized scores of them and who had later rolled around drunk in the Kootenai village and fornicated with squaws. Tonight, faced with the spectacle of this counterfeit monster, they were silent at first. Then a couple made remarks that sounded like questions, and a man in the dark honked like a goose, and people let themselves laugh at the wolf-boy.

But they hushed, all at once and quite abruptly, when he stood still at center stage, his arms straight out from his shoulders, and went rigid, and began to tremble with a massive inner dynamism. Nobody present had ever seen anyone stand so still and yet so strangely mobile. He laid his head back until his scalp contacted his spine, that far back, and opened his throat, and a sound rose in the auditorium like a wind coming from all four directions, low and terrifying, rumbling up from the ground beneath the floor, and it gathered into a roar that sucked at the hearing itself, and coalesced into a voice that penetrated into the sinuses and finally into the very minds of those hearing it, taking itself higher and higher, more and more awful and beautiful, the originating ideal of all such sounds ever made, of the foghorn and the ship's horn, the locomotive's lonesome whistle, of opera singing and the music of flutes and the continuous moan-music of bagpipes. And suddenly it all went black. And that time was gone forever.

Editing

The relationship that you have with your work of fiction will change during its development. At the beginning you are inseparable from it, in that it originates from the amorphous depths of your imagination, but as the words amass – and then are redrafted into a different course – the text begins to take a shape, a form, that is its own. It is not you; it is something that you have produced for other people to read. So ask yourself: Should you remain so faithful to the writer you were in that first heat of inspiration that you are reluctant now to change much of the material, because your vision can never be as pure as it was then? Or should you be faithful instead to the work itself, the end product?

The answer, of course, is that if you want your writing to have an impact on other people, the most important thing is the work itself.

Furthermore, it is by concentrating on making the best possible end product that you are, in fact, being most faithful to the purity of that initial vision.

Editing well is about neutralizing the artistic subjectivity that went into laying down the words in the first place.

> There are two harnessed visions that go into any piece of fiction writing: the imaginative one that you set out with, and the clear-eyed editorial vision that does it justice.

The imaginative and editorial visions cannot be put to use at the same time. They are vital, but counterweighted, endeavours. Probably the single greatest difficulty that inexperienced writers get themselves into is in trying to yoke the two: to edit as you go. So leave the editing until the material is down, redrafted by whatever method you have decided upon. And enjoy the edit. Editing your work is not a necessary chore; it is an essential part of the creative process. It makes your work better. Why would you not enjoy that?

Your editing process will shape itself differently around each individual piece of writing. By the time you reach the editing stage, you will probably know where particular emphasis might be needed, or if there are customized editing actions that pertain to a current narrative that were not necessary for a previous one. With practice, however, you will form your own set of editing principles, which you will use to guide you through each work. These generally fall into two categories: *separation* and *specificity*.

Separation

In order to perceive the text objectively – as your reader will – you need to make the experience of reading your work critically as close as possible to the experience that somebody else will have on reading it. So you need to separate your artistic self from your editorial self.

Take your time. The most effective way of becoming objective about the words you have written is by forgetting them. Try it: as an experiment, write two random, standalone scenes of fiction. (Here, if you would like them, are two prompts: *a man, alone at home, goes out into the garden and gets onto his children's trampoline; a woman, driving late at night, comes across the body of a cow, not quite dead, paralysed on the road.*)

For the purposes of the experiment, miss out any redrafting stage and revise one scene as soon as you have finished it. Leave the other scene for a month or two, then revise it. The chances are that you will make more alterations to the scene that has been left for a while, for the simple reason that it is easier to be ruthless when you have left behind the subjective intention of the sentences. And if you want your work to shine, you do need to be ruthless.

Change your working conditions. Anything that alters the particular atmosphere you created for yourself when you wrote your first draft and your redraft(s) will help you to see it with new eyes. So, if you wrote your drafts in a certain café, or library, find a different one for your edit. Or if you wrote it always in the same seat at the kitchen table, move to the opposite side of the table. Don't underestimate the influence of minute environmental factors on the psychological mechanisms that go on as you put pen to paper. Or fingers to keyboard. Which is, incidentally, another useful change – swapping between longhand and computer; it makes the text look different, so naturally you will read it differently.

Consult other people (when you are ready). There is a distinction to be made between the editing work that you do at your own behest, and that which you might do because of the advice of somebody else. All writers will benefit from the insight of a judicious editor, and it would be peevishly self-righteous to think otherwise. However, even if you are fortunate enough to know such a person, never forget that the work is yours; if you ever find yourself starting to make changes to it that you do not agree with, you are in an unhealthy situation.

Good feedback from an editor – or a friend, or another writer in a workshop setting – will cause you to reflect, and trickle that feedback into the stream of your own thoughts. This in turn will probably spur you into new ones, with the ultimate consequence of improving the writing. Never shut out other people's opinions. But at the same time, remember that the most important one is your own.

Specificity

There is a time for a general read-through (probably at the start of your edit, and many times at the end), but you will overlook most of the elements that need revision if you are trying to look for all of them at the same time. Rather than read the whole thing through ten times with the same catch-all approach, sweep through it ten times, looking each time to revise one specific thing. (By the way, the number ten here is theoretical. If you are editing rigorously, and especially if it is a novel, it's going to be a lot more than ten times. If you're only looking for one thing, though, you will be much more efficient.) Many of these editing sweeps will be related, too. So the editing work you do on a character's development, for instance, will automatically tighten the plot at the same time.

Individual works require individual edits. You will develop your own list of sweeps for each project, but here are some staple ones to consider.

Plot progression. Skim through the text and consider the through-line of plot release. Do this for the main plots, and any subplots. Because these will inevitably be interrelated, one useful method is to bullet-point all the plot events in the narrative, in order, in a separate document. And because sometimes single words will also have an effect on the plot, put these in the document too. This will give you an outline of the plot shape, which you can use to examine the narrative flow for clarity, subtlety and, importantly, pace. Are there passages of redundant filler between the significant plot events? Is the plot release brought about prematurely, or not soon enough?

Character development. Focus on each character one
by one and scrutinize whether particular attributes of their
behaviour and motivation, the intentions of which are clear
to you, will be clear to the reader. Looking through the
editing folders for my last novel, for example, it is full of
headings like: *Trace Leah's resentment through-line and how it
relates to homophobia... Trace Bobby's gambling through-line...
Consider the level of self-loathing in early Tom...*

Structure. The redraft was a natural restructuring process in
itself, in which you will have made decisions about the narrative
shape based on what you learned through the mess of the
first draft. Now, though, is another opportunity to expose and
examine the structure. The plot bullet-points document will
help with this, as will any kind of flow chart (like the one on
pages 92–93) that lays bare the parts of the novel that focus
on, for example, particular characters, or periods of time,
places, events. This flow chart will also let you see at a glance
the different chapter weightings, where section breaks occur,
dialogue and so on ... you can tailor it however you like.

Word repetition. You will know instinctively that there are
some words you have overused – whether that means two
'empurpleds', or 190 'glances'. And if you want some extra
help, most writing software has frequency detectors. Sometimes
the worn-out words will occur only in one particular narrative;
other times they might be words that an author reaches for in
book after book. The moment a reader spots the recurrence, the
fictional dream breaks.
    To this, you could add other repetition sweeps, looking
out for where you have repeated similar phrasing, sentence
structures, chapter beginnings, chapter endings, situations,
character behaviours...

Theme. If there were any thematic ideas that propelled you to write the narrative in the first instance – or any that grew out of your drafting process – read through now to analyze whether these themes are breathing powerfully enough through the text. Or, as is more common, breathing too powerfully. It is often interesting to note, however, as you revisit the text, that during the process of writing you have departed far enough from your initial thought that the narrative has become about something else entirely. Which might be the right thing for the piece; or might have diluted it. Now is the time to address that question.

Subtlety. Not just thematic, but at the sentence and scene level, too. Are there places where the thing you want to get across is too hidden, too opaque – or too blatant?

Point of view and tense. Read through looking solely for the consistency of these things. Does the tense ever switch unintentionally? Is the point of view always controlled, or are there moments when your close third person jumps clumsily into omniscient, or the other way round? (Look carefully: there probably will be.)

Elements. Go through the other chapter headings in this book. Is the opening definitely the most appropriate entry point, and does it carry the right balance of intrigue without forced attention-seeking? Read through each character's speech acts and test them for consistency. Review the language level. Is it consistent – or are there patches of stylistic deviation: flourish fires, followed by plain writing? Or areas where, even if the reader wouldn't know the reason for it, you can see perfectly well the join between that week when you finished reading *Blood Meridian* and then started *Mrs Dalloway*?

Continuity. Probe for moments of illogic and corrupted through-line, much as a film continuity editor would, making sure that the broken plant pot of one scene does not rematerialize intact in another. A film, remember, like many works of art, is the collaborative process of many people working in harmony; as a fiction writer, there is only you.

Punctuation. Obviously. Checking for accuracy, clarity, rhythmic control, stylistic tics...

Esotericism. The longer you sit with a text, the easier it can be to lose sight of the fact that some detail that might be perfectly obvious to you, because of your thorough knowledge of a subject, might be incomprehensible to the reader. Don't assume that they know everything you know. The flip side of this sweep is to find the places where you have tried too hard to explain esoteric detail to the reader and, as a consequence, made it expositional. Mediate between these two positions so that all of the subject detail arises subtly from the text, and can be absorbed naturally by the reader.

Once you embrace that truth you will be able to do it better, and take great satisfaction from the incremental improvement, tweak by tweak, of your work.

Life, writing

'That's a lot of work', you might be thinking. And it is. If you enjoy writing as a pastime, and all that you want from it is a creative outlet, that is one thing. But if you want to create something that you would like other people to read, and be affected by, then there is no sidestepping the amount of work involved. Though perhaps work is not quite the right word to use.

Pain.

Care. Craft. Scrupulousness. Endeavour.

Writing fiction is all of these.

Where 'work' *is* a useful word is in determining how dedicated you are going to be to it, this project of yours. Where does it rank in the priorities of your everyday life? I am not trying to say here that you need to make it more important than caring for your children (as I write this, mind you, I have just noticed that my five-year-old daughter is outside playing with a knife), but you need to give it status as you figure out logistically how to fit your writing into your time. In short, you need to commit to it. On the page, and off the page.

(I went outside and took the knife from her, by the way, before I finished that last sentence.)

Read as widely as you can, and read things that you would not ordinarily pick up.

> Nothing will sharpen your understanding of writing fiction more than careful reading of fiction.

Being aware of what is going on in contemporary fiction, as a contemporary fiction writer yourself, is important, alongside reading keenly and deeply from literature of the past. Modern fiction, like all art forms, is in constant flux, which is not to say that you need to follow where it is going, but that it is important to know what is happening around you.

Movements wax and wane. Read as much as you can, and be influenced by this reading, or reject it; do it your own way, founded on an awareness of yourself as a writer amongst others.

Sharing your work with people will also help, especially if that sharing is reciprocal. Asking your grandad to give it the once-over and having him tell you, 'That's smashing, that is', is all well and good, but a person who asks you to read her own work in return with the same attentiveness and objectivity will be much more helpful.

Going on a writing course is one way to meet other writers. There are many such courses available, each with its own structure and focus. Some are publishing-oriented; some are about providing time and space; some about meeting people... Think about what it is that you most need, and commit wholeheartedly.

This, though, is not a book for advice on courses, or agents, publishers or competitions. There are many other books and websites for that. The purpose of this book is to make the writing of a work of fiction seem approachable. It is a process, with many considerations; it is not magic. Nor is it something exclusive, or special. There are special works of fiction, of course – and the twenty-five on these pages are a decent starting point in your search for new material to read – but the act of writing is in itself not special.

Writing a book does not make you special.

And if ever you find yourself thinking that it is – that you are – special, then it will be a good idea to sit down and give yourself a talking to, because you have wandered away from what is really important. The project at hand is what should be special to you. It is something to be attempted seriously, in that you appreciate the amount of time and craft and rigour that will be necessary. Yet it is also something to relish – all of the surprise and vexation and possibility of it. It is something to be enjoyed.

133

From *The Wallcreeper* by Nell Zink. Copyright © 2014 by Nell Zink. Reprinted by permission of HarperCollins Publishers Ltd and the author. **111** From *A Girl is a Half-formed Thing* by Eimear McBride, 2013. First published by Galley Beggar Press, 2013. Copyright © 2013 by Eimear McBride. Reproduced by permission of Gallery Beggar Press; Coffee House Press and The Text Publishing Company. **113** From *The Driver's Seat* by Muriel Spark. Copyright © 1970 Copyright Administration Limited. Reproduced by permission of David Higham Associates Ltd. **115** From *A Heart So White* by Javier Marias, translated by Margaret Jull Costa, Penguin Books, 2012. Copyright © 1992 by Javier Marias. Translation copyright © 1995 by The Harvill Press. Reproduced by permission of Penguin Books Ltd and Vintage Books, an imprint of the Knopf Doubleday Publishing Group, a division of Penguin Random House LLC. All rights reserved. **123** From *Train Dreams* by Denis Johnson. Copyright © 2002 by Denis Johnson. Reproduced by permission of Granta Books and Farrar, Straus and Giroux.

28 © Penguin Books, 2014. **30** Courtesy of Houghton Mifflin Harcourt. **36** © Penguin Books, 1986. **38** Cover Design: Christopher Gale. Series Design: Rafaela Romaya. Reprinted by permission of Canongate Books. **46** © Penguin Books, 2000. **70** © Penguin Books, 2008. **72** Design: Peter Adlington. Cover Photography: © David Seymour/Magnum Photos. Reprinted by permission of Canongate Books. **82** Reprinted by permission of HarperCollins Publishers Ltd. **88** Reprinted by permission of HarperCollins Publishers Ltd. **94** © Penguin Books, 2012. **100** © Penguin Books, 2006. **102** Reproduced with permission of Macmillan through PLSclear. **106** Reprinted by permission of Dorothy, a publishing project. **112** Reproduced with permission of Macmillan through PLSclear. **122** Reprinted by permission of Granta Books

Ross Raisin is the author of three novels, most recently, *A Natural*, which was published to outstanding critical acclaim in 2017. His previous novels, *God's Own Country* (2008 - titled *Out Backward* in the US), and *Waterline*, won or were shortlisted for ten awards. In 2009 he was named the *Sunday Times* Young Writer of the Year, and in 2013 he was selected as one of *Granta's* Best of Young British writers. Ross lives in London, where he teaches creative writing at Goldsmiths College and is a writer-in-residence for the schools' charity First Story.

I would like to thank Sophie Drysdale and Donald Dinwiddie, along with everybody else at Laurence King involved in the making of this book. And, above all, my appreciation goes to the hundreds of writers, from the eight-year-olds to the eighty-year-olds, who have so obligingly subjected themselves to my nitpickings over the years.

What's your angle?

Get close.
And then get closer.